JESUS WINS!

Re-Reading Revelation for Young People

Virginia L. Smith, PhD

www.authorvirginiasmith.com

JESUS WIN! Re-Reading Revelation for Young People
Copyright © 2024 by Virginia L. Smith

All rights reserved. This book or any portion thereof may not be reproduced or used in any manner whatsoever without the express written permission of the author except for the use of brief quotations in a book review or scholarly journal.

The author assumes full responsibility for the accuracy of all facts and quotations as cited in this book. The opinions expressed in this book are the author's personal views and interpretations.

Self-published by Author Virginia Smith
ISBN- 979-8-9905917-0-7 (Paperback)
ISBN- 979-8-9905917-1-4 (Adobe PDF)
Cover Design by: Joshua Nguyen | GCCH-Media
Interior Design by: GCCH-Media
Illustrations by: GCCH-Media with AI tools

All Scripture quotations, unless otherwise noted, are taken from the **Holy Bible, New International Version® (NIV)**. Copyright © 1973, 1978, 1984, 2011 by Biblica, Inc.™ Used by permission of Zondervan. All rights reserved worldwide.

Printed in Thailand,
First Printing, 2024

DEDICATION

To Conrad who was tortured by the questions that only have answers in *The Revelation of Jesus Christ*.

Acknowledgments

Dr. Sigve Tonstad has provided most of the inspiration and information for this book. His careful insights have truly given me the promised revival and entirely different religious experience that were predicted in the statements at the beginning of this book. However, any mistakes in the book are entirely my own.

Sally Dillon also taught me to study the Bible with new eyes. She had a way of presenting truth to children that drew them in and gave them not just interest in the Bible, but a personal investment in being a part of God's kingdom. She died too young. I pray for her boys, Donnie and Michael, that they will remember all that she taught them.

Pastor Terry McComb in Canada told me about a mother who was looking for a way to study the book of Revelation with her children. Ideas for this were already niggling about in my head, but his words prompted me to start writing. I hope she may see this book and find it useful.

It was my beloved grandson Conrad who spurred me to finish this book. He needed the information found here to give him hope and meaning in life. It came too late for him, but I pray that those who read this book will find both.

Joshua Nguyen, a junior IT major here at Asia-Pacific International University has really made this happen by his expertise in formatting, illustrating, and publishing. It has been a joy and a privilege to work with him.

Frank and Charlene Mantiri with their children agreed to be the guinea pigs to taste and see whether this book was good. Their enthusiastic approval was a tremendous encouragement, and you can read their comments on the back cover.

My friends are my cheerleaders, and I acknowledge their helpfulness and encouragement to keep writing. They are multitude! Naming just a few is difficult to impossible. So let me just say, "You know who you are, and thank you from the bottom of my heart."

My family constantly inspires me. Jennifer and Jessica and Juliana especially tug at my heart strings and keep me moving forward. My husband Calvin has patiently accepted late meals and delayed plans as he urged me to keep writing on this project.

The dear Jesus who revealed all the mysteries found in His Revelation has been, as always, endlessly faithful in aiding me to "will and to do" (Philippians 2:13). I will close by referring once more to my favorite text which is Isaiah 26:12 NIV:

> LORD, you establish peace for us; all that we have accomplished you have done for us.

Virginia Smith
September, 2024

Table of Contents

Dedication III
Acknowledgment.. V
Note to Parents and Teachers XIII
Introduction XV

PART 1: REVELATION 1 THROUGH 3 — 1

01 John Sees His Dear Friend — 3

Revelation 1:1-3: Introduction and Blessing 3
Revelation 1:4-8: Greetings to the Churches from John and God 5
Revelation 1:9-20: In Vision, John Sees Jesus Christ.................................. 7
Symbols in Chapter One.. 11

02 Four of the Seven Churches — 13

Revelation 2:1-7: To the Angel of the Church in Ephesus, Write 14
Revelation 2:8-11: To the Angel of the Church in Smyrna, Write 15
Revelation 2:12-17: To the Angel of the Church in Pergamum, Write...... 17
Revelation 2:18-29: To the Angel of the Church in Thyatira, Write 19
Symbols in Chapter Two... 21

03 The Last Three of the Seven Churches — 23

Revelation 3:1-6: To the Angel of the Church in Sardis, Write 23
Revelation 3:7-13: To the Angel of the Church in Philadelphia, Write...... 25
Revelation 3:14-22: To the Angel of the Church in Laodicea, Write........ 26
Symbols in Chapter Three.. 29

PART II: REVELATION 4 THROUGH 7 — 31

04 In the Throne Room of the Universe — 33

05 A Big Problem in Heaven — 37

Symbols in Chapter Five... 40

06 Six Seals — 41

Revelation 6:1-2: Opening the First Seal 41
Revelation 6:3-8: Opening the Second, Third and Fourth Seals 43
Revelation 6:9-11: The Fifth Seal 50
Revelation 6:12-17 and Revelation 8:1: The Sixth and Seventh Seals ... 52
Symbols in Chapter Six 55

07 Intermission or Intervention — 59

Revelation 7:1-8: God's People Sealed 59
Revelation 7:9-17: An Innumerable Multitude In Heaven 61
Symbols in Chapter Seven 62

PART III: THE SEVEN TRUMPETS — 63

08 The Seventh Seal and the First Four Trumpets — 65

Revelation 8:1: Silence in Heaven 65
Revelation 8:2-5: The Golden Censer 66
Revelation 8:6-13: The First Four Trumpets 68
Symbols in Chapter Eight 70

09 The Fifth and Sixth Trumpets — 71

Revelation 9:1-12: The First Woe 72
Revelation 9:13-21: The Second Woe 74
Symbols in Chapter Nine 79

10 The Second Intermission — 81

Revelation 10:1-7: The Mystery of God Comes to Completion 81
Revelation 10:8-11: The Angel and the Little Scroll 84
Symbols in Chapter Ten 86

11 The Intermission and the Seventh Trumpet — 87

Revelation 11:1-2: Measuring the Temple 87
Revelation 11:3-14: The Two Witnesses 89
Revelation 11:15-19: The Seventh Trumpet 94
Symbols in Chapter Eleven 97

PART IV: THE COSMIC CONFLICT FROM A TO Z — 99

12 Part 1: The Woman and the Dragon — 101

Revelation 12:1-4: Two Great Signs 102
Revelation 12:5-6: The Baby and the Woman 102
Revelation 12:7-9: How the War Started 103
Revelation 12:10-12: A Joyful Celebration In Heaven, But Woe to the Earth 106
Revelation 12:13-17: Satan's Continuing War Against the Woman 106
Symbols in Chapter Twelve 110

13 The Big Picture of the Cosmic Conflict, Part 2 — 111

Revelation 13:1-10: The Beast from the Sea 111
Revelation 13:11-18: The Beast from the Earth 115
Symbols in Chapter Thirteen 119

14 The Big Picture of the Cosmic Conflict, Part 3 — 121

Revelation 14:6-13: The Three Angels' Messages 122
Revelation 14:14-20: The Harvest of the Earth 128
Revelation 14:1-5: The Victory Celebration 130
Symbols in Chapter Fourteen 133

PART V: THE SEVEN BOWLS — 135

15 Open Heaven — 137

Revelation 15:1-4: Singing the Song of Moses,
        the Song Also Sung by the Lamb 137
Revelation 15:5-8: Readying the Seven Bowls 139
Symbols in Chapter Fifteen 141

16 Seven Bowls of Wrath — 143

Revelation 16:1-9: The First Four Bowls 145
Revelation 16:10-16: The Fifth and Sixth Bowls 148
Revelation 16:17-21: The Seventh Bowl 151
Symbols in Chapter Sixteen 153

PART VI: REVELATION 17 AND 18 — 155

17 The Beast That Was, and Is Not, and Is to Come — 157

Revelation 17:1-7: The Angel Shows John the Great Prostitute 158
Revelation 17:8-18: The Angel Explains the Beast and the Woman 159
Symbols in Chapter Seventeen 166

18 Babylon's Fall — 167

Revelation 18:1-3: Lament Over Fallen Babylon................................... 168
Revelation 18:4-8: Warning to Escape Babylon's Judgment 169
Revelation 18:9-20: Threefold Woe Over Babylon's Fall 170
Revelation 18:21-24: The Silent City 173
Symbols in Chapter Eighteen 175

PART VII: CHAPTERS 19 THROUGH 22 — 177

19 A Huge Celebration — 179

Revelation 19:1-10: Victory Is Celebrated in Heaven with a Wedding.. 179
Revelation 19:11-16: The Last War--Armageddon 182
Revelation 19:17-21: A Picture of Wastelands 183

20 The Thousand Years — 185

Revelation 20:1-3: Satan Bound for a Thousand Years 186
Revelation 20:4-6: Judgment in Heaven During the Thousand Years .. 188
Revelation 20:7-10: Satan Released 189
Revelation 20:11-15: The Last Judgment 190

21 A New Heaven And A New Earth — 195

Revelation 21:1-8: A New Heaven and a New Earth 195
Revelation 21:9-27: The New Jerusalem, the Bride of the Lamb 197
Symbols in Chapter Twenty-One 200

22 The Glorious Conclusion — 203

Revelation 22:1-5: Eden Restored 203
Revelation 22:6-11: John and the Angel 204
Epilogue: Invitation and Warning 205

Appendix A 207
Bibliography 209
About the Author 217

NOTE TO PARENTS AND TEACHERS

> The book of Revelation, in connection with the book of Daniel, especially demands study. Let every God-fearing teacher consider how most clearly to comprehend and to present the gospel that our Savior came in person to make known to His servant John—"The Revelation of Jesus Christ, which God gave unto Him, to show unto His servants things which must shortly come to pass." Revelation 1:1. None should become discouraged in the study of the Revelation because of its apparently mystical symbols. "If any of you lack wisdom, let him ask of God, that giveth to all men liberally, and upbraideth not." James 1:5 *Education*, page 191

Ellen G. White, a profound biblical thinker, has written statements that make it clear that there is still more to learn from the book of Revelation. Don't be surprised if you find ideas written in the pages ahead that differ from what you have heard before.

> Increased light will shine upon all the grand truths of prophecy, and they will be seen in freshness and brilliancy, because the bright beams of the Sun of Righteousness will illuminate the whole. *Evangelism*, page 198

> When we as a people understand what this book (Revelation) means to us, there will be seen among us a great revival. We do not understand fully the lessons that it teaches, notwithstanding the injunction given to search and study it. *Testimonies to Ministers*, page 113

> When the books of Daniel and Revelation are better understood, believers will have an entirely different religious experience. *Testimonies to Ministers*, page 114

Introduction

It is wonderful that Jesus came in person to make the gospel known to the Apostle John. And we can understand the meaning of the book of Revelation by the wisdom God is happy to supply. Let's be sure to always emphasize the gospel as we study Revelation.

God is love (1 John 4:8). We know that because the Bible is full of stories and promises to show that He is love. Hopefully we are also aware of that love in our lives. And we need to remember His love all the time we are studying His book, Revelation. The most famous Bible verse about God's love is John 3:16. Probably you have memorized it.

> *For God so loved the world that he gave His one and only Son, that whoever believes in Him shall not perish but have eternal life.*

This verse was written by the Apostle John, Jesus' youngest disciple. Maybe you remember that he was very special to Jesus. He referred to himself as the one who Jesus loved.[1] After Jesus went back to heaven the Apostle John lived longer than any other of Jesus' disciples.

When he was very old, he was the spiritual leader of several Christian churches that were in the country we now call Turkey. It was a part of the Roman Empire, and the government did not appreciate Christians because they would not pray to the emperor who was considered to be a god. Since John was the leader, they decided to kill him by putting him in a big kettle of boiling oil. They thought that would teach a good lesson to other Christians who did not agree to their kind of worship.

God intervened so the hot oil did not hurt John at all. That must have been a very big surprise! Now what could they do? They still wanted to punish him, so they sent him to a little island named Patmos that was about 50 miles out in the water away from Ephesus, the city where he lived.

On Patmos John was supposed to work in a mine. Since he was about 90 years old, that must have been very hard for him. We know he had some freedom because we will find him enjoying nature on a Sabbath day, or maybe he was hiding in a cave that people can still visit on that island. On a clear night he might have been able to see lights from Ephesus. The church members he knew and loved were there. I'm sure he thought about them and prayed for them every day.

---

[1] *John 19:26 and other places*

Where was God while His faithful disciple John was struggling on that little island? In this book you will find the answer to that question. In fact, you will see that God was taking very good care of him. Maybe God arranged for John to be there so he would have time away from his home and church work to write an important message to you and me that he would have been too busy to write over in Ephesus living his normal life.

Most of the best scholarship believes that John wrote The Revelation of Jesus Christ about A.D. 95. The very next year, the Roman emperor was killed, so John only had a short time to write before he was liberated from Patmos and returned home to Ephesus. Later he wrote The Gospel According to John which is thought to be the last book of the Bible to be written. At some point late in his life he also wrote 1st, 2nd & 3rd John.

Thanks to John's time on Patmos, we have the book, Revelation. Have you tried to read it? Some people say it is very hard to understand. Some people say it is so hard it will drive you crazy to try to understand it. I hope you will find that is not true, that you can read and understand it, and love Jesus more because of what He reveals in it, and what it reveals about Him.

In order to understand Revelation, you only have to do three things.

1. Re-read it prayerfully

2. Pay attention to the Old Testament references

3. Recognize that God is not the only power at work

As you go through this book, you will see the good sense of these three requirements. Each of them will help you understand the meaning of Revelation. I think you will find that it is the most exciting book in the whole Bible. When you understand it, it will change your life.

Two thousand years ago, back in John's time, Greek was the language used, so that is the language John wrote in, even though he also knew the Hebrew language very well. If you want to read Revelation in the language in which John originally wrote it, you will need to learn Greek. I would encourage you to do this. When a book is translated into another language, like English, there are ideas that you could miss. For this reason, some Greek words will be explained to you as you go through this book.

It is my prayer that you will be exceedingly blessed as you study Jesus Wins! Re-reading Revelation for Young People

PART 1
REVELATION
1 THROUGH 3

Jesus' disciple John, who we know as the Apostle John, was a prisoner of the Roman Empire on the island of Patmos when his dear friend Jesus came to visit. He gave him an important vision of events stretching far into the future, as well as going way back in time.

As John spent his days working hard in the mine, his thoughts undoubtedly turned continually to the churches he loved. He had lived for a long time in Ephesus and was the spiritual leader of a circle of Christian churches. John was thinking about those churches, praying for them, and wondering how they were. Were they safe? Were they brave enough to be faithful to Jesus, no matter what happened?

Jesus knew what John was thinking, so He began the vision with messages for the churches. But the purpose of the messages to the believers was much more than just to give comfort to John. God's people are the ones who share with the world the truth of God's love and His plans to restore the world to the perfection it had at Creation. They are a most important part of Jesus' winning the war for this world.

Re-reading is necessary in studying the book of Revelation, because you need to keep in mind the whole story in order to understand its parts. Already in chapter 1, John makes references to information you won't find until you reach the very end of the book. But you may have already heard about that information. You probably know something about it from hearing or reading or studying in the past. In that sense, you are already a re-reader. That means you are in good shape to continue your study of Revelation.

If you have some negative ideas about the book, you may need to change your mind. In that sense, someone who reads this book with no idea at all about Revelation may be better prepared to start to read and re-read. Either way, re-reading will lead you to truth as you study this vision God sent to help His people understand what has happened and what is happening in the world around us.

Many think of Revelation as the sequel to the Old Testament book of Daniel. God revealed through Daniel—that he wrote into chapter 2—what would happen from his time to the end of the world. Then Daniel chapter seven added more details. Chapter eight added more details yet. Chapter nine added details about Jesus' first coming. Chapter 11 added more details again, about actual historic individuals. Once God has declared what will happen in the future, the story does not change. Revelation, this vision God gave to John, again gives many more details without changing any of the information revealed to Daniel.

In addition to Daniel, several other Old Testament books make major contributions to Revelation. Maybe the book of Isaiah adds the most of all. As we continue through the book, you will also see other names from the Old Testament. All 2,000 plus quotations that John added—sometimes just a word or a phrase—will help you to understand the meaning of Revelation.

God wants His people to understand what He is planning and what is going on in the fulfillment of His plans. That is what we will find as we go through Revelation.

CHAPTER 1
John Sees His Dear Friend

Revelation 1:1-3: Introduction and Blessing

> *1 The revelation from Jesus Christ, which God gave him to show his servants what must soon take place. He made it known by sending his angel to his servant John...*

Today you can visit the Island of Patmos and stand on the hill where John probably sat when Jesus visited him and told him to write a book. John was going to experience a long vision with a prophecy about what had happened in the past, as well as what would happen from his day down to the end of time when there would be a new heaven and a new earth.

He begins by telling us how the message was sent:

- God gave the message
- To Jesus who witnessed by passing it on

Jesus Wins! 3

- To an angel who helped deliver it
- To John who wrote it
- To be read in the churches that received it

We need to think about the word "revelation." When you see or hear that word, what do you think it means? You probably realize you are going to see or learn something you did not see or learn before. It is like curtains being pulled back so you can see what is happening on the stage behind the curtains.

The Greek word that is translated as "revelation" sounds very much like our English word "apocalypse." Today we think of that word meaning a disaster, or a catastrophe. Actually, it meant to take the lid off a box to reveal something that had been hidden inside. As we continue through our study of Revelation, we need to keep in mind this meaning of the word.

Also, when there is a revelation, there has to be a revealer. Someone is making it possible for you to see and learn what is going on. Someone is pulling back the curtains. Someone is taking the lid off the box. Who is that Someone in this case?

The first sentence begins with, "The revelation *from* Jesus Christ. . .". In the Greek language, that can mean the message came from Jesus or is about Him. Or it can mean both. As you read this book you will find that, indeed, it is both. Jesus had many things to reveal to us, and in the process, we learn many things about Him.

A very important word in the first verse is lost in the New International Version of the Bible that simply says, "He made it known by sending His angel." Jesus sent an angel to help pass on the vision to John on Patmos. In Greek, and in the New King James Version of the Bible, it says He sent and "signified" it by His angel to John. In the Greek language,[2] the word "signified" means that this vision, this prophecy, was given in symbols. Much of what you read in Revelation is intended to refer to something different from what it says. For instance, when you read about grasshoppers, the book is really talking about something else, not real grasshoppers. You can expect lots of symbols. That is partly why this book is so exciting.

Why do you think Jesus is going to use a lot of symbols? We can't be positively sure, but here are a couple of suggestions. You may think of

---
[2] *Be sure to read what the Introduction says about Greek words*

other reasons. First of all, symbols make the book more interesting, like a puzzle. There are easy puzzles that you do once and have no interest in doing again. Then there are hard puzzles that keep you thinking for a long time to figure them out.

Jesus knew that people would need to study Revelation for many years before all of the prophecy came to pass, so the book needed to be hard enough to keep them interested in studying it. If it were too easy, nobody would want to read it more than once.

Another possible reason is because many bad things were going to happen in the years ahead. Many people would want to hurt God's children. By using symbols, Jesus made it almost impossible for the bad people to understand what God was planning and doing. That way, His people, His children, would be much safer.

If you think of another reason for symbols, write a note in the margin of this page. That way, you won't forget it.

In verse 3, John gives an introduction and promises that anyone who studies and believes this prophecy would be blessed. That includes you. You can expect to be blessed as you read this book.

Revelation 1:4--8: Greetings to the Churches from John and God

> *4 John,*
>
> *To the seven churches in the province of Asia:*
>
> *Grace and peace to you from him who is, and who was, and who is to come, and from the seven spirits before his throne,*
>
> *5 and from Jesus Christ, who is the faithful witness, the firstborn from the dead, and the ruler of the kings of the earth.*

In verse 4, John gave his own name so others would know who was writing the book or scroll. All the churches knew exactly who he was, and Christian writers close to the time he lived have written that this John was the disciple, the Apostle, the brother of James, the son of Zebedee. We can be confident that he is the same John we read about in the Gospels.

Next, he wrote greetings to the churches he knew and loved so well. He used a typical Greek greeting: "Grace." And he added a typical Hebrew greeting: "Peace." The greetings he gave came from God the Father, from the Holy Spirit, and from Jesus who is God the Son. You can see that this greeting to the churches came from all three persons of the Divine Trinity. The Holy Spirit is referred to as the seven spirits before God's throne, because seven is the symbol for perfection.

John writes three different titles for Jesus:

- ▶ The faithful witness: Jesus faithfully witnessed about His Father when He lived on this earth, and He will faithfully witness God's message as He gives it to John in this vision.

- ▶ The firstborn from the dead: This does not mean Jesus was the first person ever to rise from the dead. Moses, Lazarus and others rose from the dead before He did. In Old Testament times the first-born son was the one who received the birthright. That meant he was the most important, he inherited more than his siblings, and he was the family priest and in charge of the family after his father. Jesus is the most important person to rise from the dead. In fact, if he had not risen from the dead, nobody else would ever be able to be resurrected.

- ▶ The ruler of the kings of the earth: Kings may think that nobody is higher in position than they are, but actually, all of them are subject to God the Son who will hold them accountable for what they do. God the Father put Jesus Christ in charge of everything and everyone in this sinful world.

Next, John wrote a tribute of praise to Jesus:

> *5 To him who loves us and has freed us from our sins by his blood,*
>
> *6 and has made us to be a kingdom and priests to serve his God and Father—to him be glory and power for ever and ever! Amen.*

In verse 7, John wrote very interesting information about Jesus Christ that would happen far into the future. When you and I read usual books today, we don't know what will happen at the end of the book. It is a surprise most of us wait to learn about when we finish reading the book.

In Bible times, God knew that people liked to understand what was going to happen at the end. Then they could think about all the parts of the story leading up to the end. So, God led John to reveal the end of the story first.

Verse 7:

- Look He is coming with the clouds
- and every eye will see Him
- even those who pierced Him
- and all people on earth will mourn because of Him.
- So shall it be! Amen.

Verse 8 is a message from God the Father: "I am the Alpha (the first letter of the Greek alphabet) and the Omega (the last letter of the Greek alphabet), says the Lord God, 'who is, and who was and who is to come, the Almighty.'" God is in full control of the past, the present and the future.

After reading these verses, you should never feel like Jesus is the only one in heaven who loves and cares for you.

Revelation 1:9-20: In Vision, John Sees Jesus Christ

> *9 I, John, your brother and companion in the suffering and kingdom and patient endurance that are ours in Jesus, was on the island of Patmos because of the word of God and the testimony of Jesus.*

When John says he is their companion in the suffering and kingdom and patient endurance, he is talking about the fact that living in the kingdom of Rome as a Christian, the readers could expect persecution of various kinds. He was a prisoner working in a mine. Others would also experience various trials because they loved Jesus and His word enough to endure whatever happened to them.

In this early part of the book, it reads as though maybe John thinks he is only writing for his churches. Maybe he had not yet discovered that this book would be terribly important for all God's people to study until Jesus comes back to take us home with Him.

Soon, he will be writing as though he knows he is writing the last book of the Bible. That makes sense because he was the last disciple living who had walked and talked with Jesus.

John introduced himself and connected his experience to the experience of his friends in the churches. He mentioned where he was and why he was there. On a Sabbath—the Day of the Lord—he was praying and thinking about God when suddenly he heard a loud voice behind him telling him to write what he sees, and then to send the scroll to be read in the seven churches that he knows and loves. Because in the Bible the number seven is a symbol for totality and perfection, these churches represent all of God's churches throughout time. These messages are for us as well as for those specific churches. It is through the communities of God's people that Jesus is going to win, to be triumphant.

I think Jesus was aware of John's concern for those churches and wanted to ease his mind about them, as well as to show John how important His people are and will continue to be. It is God's communities of faith who will fulfill the mission of taking the Gospel to the world.

When John turned around to see who was speaking, he saw seven lampstands. This is the next symbol we come to in the book. And it introduces us to something very important throughout John's book. The symbols are almost always closely tied to stories in the Old Testament. That was the Bible until the New Testament was written and approved as inspired by God. The Old Testament was the Bible that both Jesus and John read and studied. And John will use references to the Old Testament at least 2000 times as he is writing Revelation.

When you think of lampstands, what do you remember from the Old Testament? The tabernacle tent that was built near Mt. Sinai had seven lamps that were all on one lampstand.[3] But when Solomon built the temple, it had 10 lampstand.[4] In both places, the lamps were a source of light in a sanctuary—the place where God was with His people. Before we come to the end of Revelation 1, we will read the exact meaning of these lampstands.

Among the lampstands in the sanctuary, John saw an amazing person who he says is like a son of man. Remember that that was a phrase Jesus liked to use about Himself.[5] In verses 12 through 16, John uses several different words to describe how this Person looked:

---

[3] *Exodus 25:31-39*

[4] *1 Kings 7:48-49*

[5] *The term, Son of man, is used by Jesus 80 times as a way to refer to himself (32 times in Matthew; 14 times in Mark; 26 times in Luke; and 10 times in John)*

- a linen robe with a golden sash
- white like wool
- white as snow
- blazing fire
- bronze glowing in a furnace
- the sun shining in all its brilliance

Also, "His voice was like the sound of rushing waters. In His right hand He held seven stars and out of His mouth came a sharp double-edged sword."

Here we have more symbols. We'll come back to these a bit later.

In the Old Testament, descriptions like this are always visions of God. In Daniel 7:9-10, the Ancient of Days is described in similar ways. In Daniel 10:5-6, the vision of Jesus is almost the same.

When John saw this beautiful, majestic person, what happened to him at that moment? He was so frightened he fell down at the feet of the Person as though he were dead. Then what happened?

The shining Person placed His right hand on John and said, "Don't be afraid." How many stories can you think of from the Old Testament where an angel or Jesus appeared to someone, and it frightened them? Then the first thing said is usually, "Don't be afraid."

Now, in verses 17 and 18, the Person introduced Himself:

- I am the First and the Last
- I am the Living One
- I was dead, and now look,
- I am alive for ever and ever!
- I hold the keys of death and Hades.

At what point do you think John realized that this was Jesus, His dear friend from long years ago? He looked totally different than John remembered him, except for the time they were together on the Mount of Transfiguration.[6]

---

[6] *Matthew 17:1-6; Mark 9:2-8*

By now he surely recognized Him, and Jesus repeated the instruction to write down what he sees. Twelve times throughout the book, John is instructed to "Write." Some of what he saw took place right then, but much took place in the past and much more would happen through the centuries until Jesus comes the second time in power and glory, and then beyond that to the New Earth.

In verse 20, Jesus reveals the meaning of two of the symbols:

The seven stars that He holds are the angels of the seven churches. Maybe this means Jesus is caring for the pastors of the churches. Maybe it means there are literal angels who help each church. Either way, it means Jesus is intimately involved with the churches. He is holding on to them.

The seven lampstands are the seven churches. In the Old Testament, the lampstands were in a sanctuary. Now, and in John's day, people worship God in a church which is sometimes called a sanctuary. And the church is the source of light for its community. We can be sure that by His Spirit, Jesus is involved in all our churches.

John could rest easy knowing that the churches he loved and missed were being cared for in his absence. And maybe he had begun to realize that they played a major role in the mission planned for the rest of the history of this sinful world.

Before we leave this chapter, it is good to cover a couple points. The number 7 is used in the Bible as the symbol of completeness or perfection. Here we have seven churches. I'm sure that was not all the churches there were in John's day, but by using seven churches to illustrate all the churches, Jesus shows His care for each one.

Before we go on to Revelation chapter 2, we need to think about one more symbol. What's with the sharp, double-edged sword coming out of Jesus' mouth? We need to look at other places in the Bible for help with understanding this.

The first is in the armor of God that Paul wrote about in Ephesians 6:17. There, we read that the sword of the Spirit is the word of God. The second place is Hebrews 4:12 where we read that "...the word of God is alive and active. Sharper than any double-edged sword..." The third is found near the end of the book of Revelation, in chapter 19, verse 15; "Coming out of his mouth is a sharp sword..." So, the sword is the word of God and Jesus has it coming out of His mouth in both Revelation 1:16 and 19:15.

We can conclude that the sword in Jesus' mouth is not for killing people but for giving the testimony from God. It is truth, because God only speaks truth. The important point here is that we will see that using words of truth is the way God chooses to fight against evil.

Symbols in Chapter One:

- **Alpha and Omega:** the first and the last letters of the Greek alphabet. In English they are A and Z. When used about God it refers to the fact that He is eternal. He has existed forever and will continue to exist forever.

- **Number 7:** symbolizes perfection and totality

- **Seven Spirits before His throne:** symbolize the fulness of the Holy Spirit, showing the unity among the three perfect members of the Trinity. All three of them are united in sending the message of love to God's people.

- **The seven angels of the churches:** symbolize the leaders of all God's communities of faith, or maybe all the literal angels that help and guide those groups

- **Seven golden lampstands:** symbolize the communities of faith. Just as the lampstands in the sanctuary and the temple gave light by the oil poured into them, so the groups of believers provide light to the world around them through the power of the Holy Spirit.

- **The double-edged sword in Jesus' mouth:** symbolizes truth, and the mouth symbolizes words. Jesus fights with words of truth instead of with lethal weapons. This will be an important idea as we move forward in future chapters.

CHAPTER 2
FOUR OF THE SEVEN CHURCHES

For two thousand years, Bible students have studied the seven churches that begin in Revelation, chapter 2. Some of them have seen that the ancient seven cities resembled the information given about them in the vision. I would encourage you to read one of the books that have been written with that viewpoint.

You can also visit all seven cities today (or watch videos about them on YouTube). Some are big, some are small. Some have Roman ruins you can visit. Huge amphitheaters, temples and streets and other artifacts remain from the time when the Apostle John walked there, visiting the Christian communities. Some of the towns have little or nothing left from Roman times.

In this book you will find a different approach to the study of the churches. In John's vision we will see, to our surprise, that no real attention is paid to the cities themselves, or to the Roman Empire. Each message is about the church community and what those believers were experiencing and believing and feeling. We will pay attention to that.

Remember that Jesus was among the seven golden lampstands, which means that He was with all the Christian communities. His Spirit and His angels are always close to each of us, no matter what we might be going through.

You will find that each of the seven parts of the vision follow the same pattern:

- **to whom the message is given**
- **from Whom the message comes, using part of the description of Jesus in Revelation 1**
- **a diagnoses of the condition of each church**
- **counsel in the form of a prescription**
- **a call to hear the message**
- **and finally, a promise for each church taken from the images in Revelation 20 to 22**

The call is interesting, because all seven churches receive exactly the same call: "Whoever has ears, let them hear what the Spirit says to the churches." That means that if you have ears, you are called to hear what the Spirit says to the churches. There is something here for you. Think about that as we look at the seven messages.

Revelation 2:1-7, To the Angel of the Church in Ephesus, Write:

> *1 These are the words of Him who holds the seven stars in His right hand and walks among the seven golden lampstands.*
>
> *2 I know your deeds, your hard work and your perseverance. I know that you cannot tolerate wicked people, that you have tested those who claim to be apostles but are not, and have found them false.*
>
> *3 You have persevered and have endured hardships for my name, and have not grown weary.*

> *4 Yet I hold this against you: You have forsaken the love you had at first.*
>
> *5 Consider how far you have fallen! Repent and do the things you did at first. If you do not repent, I will come to you and remove your lampstand from its place.*
>
> *6 But you have this in your favor: You hate the practices of the Nicolaitans, which I also hate.*
>
> *7 Whoever has ears, let them hear what the Spirit says to the churches. To the one who is victorious, I will give the right to eat from the tree of life, which is in the paradise of God.*

In verses 2 and 3, the message shows how well God knows His people in Ephesus. He affirms them for their work and their attitude. Verse 4 expresses His concern that they have lost the love they had when they first became Christians. Without love, all their good traits are in danger of being worth nothing.

In verse 5, His counsel, His prescription, is for them to remember how things used to be, repent, and return to their original ways of feeling and doing, or there will be dire consequences. Not that He wants to punish them, but because without love, it becomes impossible for any of us to live for God.

Verse 6 is something different for which God affirms them. They and God hate the Nicolaitans. We don't know for sure who that is, but obviously it is some very negative influence on the church.

After the sentence about ears, the promise for victorious Ephesians is that they will be able to eat from the tree of life. I'm sure you remember the tree of life from the Garden of Eden in Genesis 2 and 3. Probably you know it will also be in heaven and in the new earth. We will come to that in the final chapters of Revelation.

Revelation 2:8-11: To the Angel of the Church in Smyrna, Write:

> *8 These are the words of Him who is the First and the Last, who died and came to life again.*

> *9 I know your afflictions and your poverty—yet you are rich! I know about the slander of those who say they are Jews and are not, but are a synagogue of Satan.*
>
> *10 Do not be afraid of what you are about to suffer. I tell you, the devil will put some of you in prison to test you, and you will suffer persecution for ten days. Be faithful, even to the point of death, and I will give you life as your victor's crown.*
>
> *11 Whoever has ears, let them hear what the Spirit says to the churches. The one who is victorious will not be hurt at all by the second death.*

In verses 8 to 11, God assured His community of believers in Smyrna that He knows their situation. Who is the first person ever to have endured slander? The answer is (drum roll): Jesus.

Long before the creation of this world, Lucifer in heaven began to spread false stories. He has never stopped. Nobody can possibly understand slander better than Jesus. He can totally empathize with the people of Smyrna who were enduring persecution and slander.

In verse 10, Jesus tells them not to be afraid of what they will suffer. He even tells them what will happen to some of them.

In both verses 9 and 10, Jesus revealed that terribly negative influences were around them and behind their sufferings. It was not the Jews, although some of the persecutors wrongly claimed to be Jews. It was the synagogue of Satan, and it was the devil who would put some of them in prison. The message did not urge them to leave for a better place; instead, Jesus counseled them to be faithful to God where they were.

When you compare life today with how long Methuselah and others lived (969 years[7]), life on earth today is not long. But no matter how long it is, Jesus promises to surround us with His care, and then He promises that those who are victorious will not be hurt at all by the second death.

Do you know about the second death? If not, stay tuned. It will be explained later in Revelation. In the meantime, verse 11 makes it clear that it will not affect those who are faithful to Jesus. This is one of the reasons

---

[7] *Genesis 5*

why it is important to read Revelation more than just once. Later parts of the book will often help you understand what you are reading in earlier parts of the book.

Revelation 2:12-17: To the Angel of the Church in Pergamum, Write:

12 These are the words of Him who has the sharp, double-edged sword.

13 I know where you live—where Satan has his throne. Yet you remain true to my name. You did not renounce your faith in me, not even in the days of Antipas, my faithful witness, who was put to death in your city—where Satan lives.

14 Nevertheless, I have a few things against you: There are some among you who hold to the teaching of Balaam, who taught Balak to entice the Israelites to sin so that they ate food sacrificed to idols and committed sexual immorality.

15 Likewise, you also have those who hold to the teaching of the Nicolaitans.

16 Repent therefore! Otherwise, I will soon come to you and will fight against them with the sword of my mouth.

17 Whoever has ears, let them hear what the Spirit says to the churches. To the one who is victorious, I will give some of the hidden manna. I will also give that person a white stone with a new name written on it, known only to the one who receives it.

Remember that the sharp, double-edged sword is the symbol for truth. Everything Jesus says is true. Continuing in verse 13, He made it clear that He understood that the Christians in Pergamum lived in a very difficult place. They lived where Satan had his throne.

We need to think about that. We know what Jesus says is always true, but maybe He is exaggerating or using hyperbole. If your mother tells you,

"I love you to death," is she exaggerating? Of course, because she is not going to kill you. People, even God, use exaggeration to make a strong point.

Satan has his leadership in many places, probably all places. But obviously, from this verse, we know that he had a particularly powerful influence in Pergamum.

According to early Christian writers, the Apostle John ordained Antipas to be the pastor in Pergamum. At some point he was executed for casting out demons that the local population worshiped. Antipas must have been remembered as a beloved person by the Christian believers. It would have been natural for them to wonder why God allowed his death to happen. But verse 13 affirms them for keeping their faith in Jesus even during that difficult time.

Unfortunately, Jesus' diagnosis had to report that Satan's influence had had an effect on the community of Christians in Pergamum. Balaam of the Old Testament did not live there, but his name makes us think of his story[8] where he was so covetous that he would do anything to get the reward the king was promising him in exchange for cursing God's people.

Then, when he could not curse them, he devised a way to lead them into sin so they would lose God's protection. His name is a very negative symbol used in the vision to describe the sins that had taken hold in this church.

Unlike the Ephesians, there were some in Pergamum who believed the teachings of the Nicolaitans. Whatever they were, we read in verse 6 that God hated those ideas.

The counsel given is for them to repent. God loves them and wants to be able to bless them. His truth (the sword) can make the difference for them.

After the instruction to listen and pay attention to God's message, the promise for them was some of the hidden manna. Maybe that means God would provide for their daily needs. Since it is hidden, it does not mean that manna would literally fall on the ground for them to pick up each day as had happened for the Israelites in the desert.[9]

In addition, God would give those who repented a white stone with a secret name written on it. Nobody else would know that name. Maybe it will be a nickname that God uses just for them to show His love.

---

[8] *Numbers 22 – 24, 31:7 - 8*
[9] *Exodus 16:4-5*

Revelation 2:18-29: To the Angel of the Church in Thyatira, Write:

18 These are the words of the Son of God, whose eyes are like blazing fire and whose feet are like burnished bronze.

19 I know your deeds, your love and faith, your service and perseverance, and that you are now doing more than you did at first.

20 Nevertheless, I have this against you: You tolerate that woman Jezebel, who calls herself a prophet. By her teaching she misleads my servants into sexual immorality and the eating of food sacrificed to idols.

21 I have given her time to repent of her immorality, but she is unwilling.

22 So I will cast her on a bed of suffering, and I will make those who commit adultery with her suffer intensely, unless they repent of her ways.

23 I will strike her children dead. Then all the churches will know that I am he who searches hearts and minds, and I will repay each of you according to your deeds.

24 Now I say to the rest of you in Thyatira, to you who do not hold to her teaching and have not learned Satan's so-called deep secrets, 'I will not impose any other burden on you,

25 except to hold on to what you have until I come.'

26 To the one who is victorious and does my will to the end, I will give authority over the nations—

27 that one will rule them with an iron scepter and will dash them to pieces like pottery—just as I have received authority from my Father.

28 I will also give that one the morning star.

29 Whoever has ears, let them hear what the Spirit says to the churches.

The people of Thyatira could believe these words because they came from the divine Son of God. He used to walk along the dusty roads in Judea and Galilee, but now He was the resplendent ruler in heaven who still cared about them and sent them this message. God knew everything about these good-hearted people. He praised them for their hard work and the improvements they had made.

Unfortunately, He also knew the bad things that were happening in their midst. His diagnosis was very serious. The stories of Jezebel in the Old Testament show that she was just about the worst person who lived among God's people. Her name is used here as a symbol of great evil that those in Thyatira were dealing with. God rebuked them for tolerating her. He knew exactly what was going on, and He revealed how He intended to deal with it.

Anyone choosing to engage in such sins would suffer sickness and lose their children unless they changed their minds and their behavior. Everyone seeing those consequences would understand that nothing is hidden from God. He knows exactly what is going on. There are consequences for whatever choices are made. God probably does not send the consequences. Sin is like poison; it brings its own consequences. When we are not on God's side, we are removing ourselves from His care and protection.

In verse 24, Jesus' message turns to all the believers who were not choosing to follow the sinful ways. Also, these faithful members had not learned Satan's deep secrets. Probably that means they did not agree to learn about spiritualistic secrets such as magic and other occult ideas that would supposedly give them great powers. Remember that Satan promised Eve greater wisdom if she would be on His side.[10]

The only counsel for those of Thyatira is to hold on to what they have—their love and faith and persevering in good deeds--until Jesus comes the second time. They lived in such a difficult place that no extra burden is put on them.

The promise to those who remain faithful and are victorious is that they would have authority over the nations. In the Bible, the nations almost always refer to places that do not follow God's ways.

Verse 27 is quoted from Psalm 2:9. At first glance it sounds like the Christians would do violent, evil things, maybe like revenge for the bad things that had been done to them. But that is not the meaning here.

---

[10] *Genesis 3:5*

The rod of iron was carried by shepherds to protect the sheep from all dangers. This promise is talking about the time when God's people will finally be free from any kind of danger. "... dash them to pieces like pottery" refers to those who face final destruction. When pottery is dashed to pieces, it is completely destroyed. It cannot be put back together.

They also receive a another promise. He will give them the morning star.[11] They will receive Jesus! What a blessing after the world of sin and darkness in which they had lived.

This brings us to the end of Revelation chapter 2. We have looked at four of the seven messages to the people of God. In each one we saw that God was with them and loved them. He knew all about them and knew exactly what they needed in order to be faithful to Him. To each of them He gave wonderful promises that will be fulfilled when He comes to take them to live with Him in heaven.

In the next chapter we will complete Part 1 by studying the last three messages John wrote and delivered to the churches.

Symbols in Chapter Two:

- **The Nicolaitans:** symbolize a group that were a bad influence on God's people

- **A synagogue of Satan:** symbolizes the people who were fighting against those who were faithful to God

- **Ten days of persecution:** Many times in the Old Testament, the words day and year were used interchangeably. Here it must mean years. We don't find information in ancient sources that there was general persecution of all Christians at that time, but at least Smyrna was facing persecution in the future.

- **Satan's throne:** symbolizes a center for worshiping Satan

- **The teaching of Balaam:** Review the story of Balaam who was so eager for reward that he tried to curse God's people. Numbers 22-24; Deuteronomy 23:4, 5. See what happened to him in Numbers 31:8. The same attitude he had was making an impact among the church members in Pergamum.

---

[11] See 22:16; Daniel 12:3

- **Manna:** God fed the people of Israel with the food of heaven the forty years they were in the desert. Exodus 16:13-15; Joshua 6:12. He promised to provide for the daily needs of Thyatira as well.
- **Jezebel:** the wicked Old Testament Sidonian queen, the wife of King Ahab, the mother of Queen Athaliah. She killed God's prophets and Naboth, fought against Elijah and was a bad influence on her husband and children. 1 Kings 16, 18, 19, 21; 2 Kings 8:18, 27; 2 Chronicles 22:2-4, 10-12
- **Iron scepter or iron rod:** quoted from Psalm 2:9 where it is referring to the metal rod a shepherd carried to protect his sheep from harm
- **Pottery dashed to pieces:** symbolizes the fate of those who face final destruction. When pottery is dashed to pieces, it is completely destroyed. It cannot be put back together.

CHAPTER 3
THE LAST THREE OF THE SEVEN CHURCHES

Revelation 3:1-6: To the Angel of the Church in Sardis, Write:

> *1 These are the words of him who holds the seven Spirits of God and the seven stars. I know your deeds; you have a reputation of being alive, but you are dead.*
>
> *2 Wake up! Strengthen what remains and is about to die, for I have found your deeds unfinished in the sight of my God.*
>
> *3 Remember, therefore, what you have received and heard; hold it fast, and repent. But if you do not wake up, I will come like a thief, and you will not know at what time I will come to you.*

> *4 Yet you have a few people in Sardis who have not soiled their clothes. They will walk with me, dressed in white, for they are worthy.*
>
> *5 The one who is victorious will, like them, be dressed in white. I will never blot out the name of that person from the book of life, but will acknowledge that name before my Father and his angels.*
>
> *6 Whoever has ears, let them hear what the Spirit says to the churches.*

This introduction to the message was to assure the Christians that God not only sends the message, He provides the means to accept it. They are in His loving hands.

Remember that the number 7 represents perfection. The seven Spirits of God is the Holy Spirit who is complete and perfect in His place and ministry in the divine Trinity.

For this church, instead of starting with affirmation, the message launches right into the diagnosis and the counsel. "You are not doing as well as you think you are. Wake up! Think about what you are doing! Remember what you have learned; repent and return to the truth."

This is urgent, because when Jesus comes again it is important that His people be awake and ready. Nobody knows when the second coming will take place. Even Jesus said He did not know.[12] And none of us knows for sure how long we will live. If we have sincerely committed our lives to Jesus, we are ready. We don't need to worry about whether we are good enough. We rely on Jesus to cover us with His righteousness.

Verse 4 says there were a few faithful people in Sardis. The promise is for them and for all God's people. They will be dressed in white robes—they will be covered with Christ's righteousness—and their names will be written in the book of life. That means they are sure of being with Jesus forever.

He is their personal representative, like their lawyer, to speak in their behalf before God and the angels. This language is referring to the coming judgment. For those who are on God's side and are waiting faithfully

---

[12] *Matthew 24:36*

for Him, the judgment is totally good news. Daniel 7:18, 22 assures us everything will finally turn out well when we are on God's side.

Just like in the message to Thyatira, the instruction to listen and pay attention comes at the very end.

Revelation 3:7-13: To the Angel of the Church in Philadelphia, Write:

> *7 These are the words of Him who is holy and true, who holds the key of David. What He opens no one can shut, and what He shuts no one can open.*
>
> *8 I know your deeds. See, I have placed before you an open door that no one can shut. I know that you have little strength, yet you have kept my word and have not denied my name.*
>
> *9 I will make those who are of the synagogue of Satan, who claim to be Jews though they are not, but are liars— I will make them come and fall down at your feet and acknowledge that I have loved you.*
>
> *10 Since you have kept my command to endure patiently, I will also keep you from the hour of trial that is going to come on the whole world to test the inhabitants of the earth.*
>
> *11 I am coming soon. Hold on to what you have, so that no one will take your crown.*
>
> *12 The one who is victorious I will make a pillar in the temple of my God. Never again will they leave it. I will write on them the name of my God and the name of the city of my God, the new Jerusalem, which is coming down out of heaven from my God; and I will also write on them my new name.*
>
> *13 Whoever has ears, let them hear what the Spirit says to the churches.*

This description of Jesus shows the character of the One who is guiding this group of Christians. He is also the One who holds the key. No matter what other people around them were saying, He is the only One who can control access to the open door of salvation and eternal life.

He holds the door open for the Philadelphians. They were weak, but they were faithful. They were doing all they could for the mission of Christ. They were being persecuted by the synagogue of Satan, just like in Smyrna. God says He has plans to turn that around and make it clear to the evildoers that He loves His believers in Philadelphia.

The counsel is for them to hold on to what they have. Jesus is coming soon.

They receive a whole series of promises, six in all, which is interesting because they are the sixth church to receive a message.

- Because they have patiently endured the persecution, God will rescue them from the hour of trial that is coming on the whole world. In other words, the time of trouble would not yet happen in their day.
- Because they have held on, they will receive a crown.
- They will be a pillar in the temple of God. They were weak when they received this message, but they will be very strong in the future.
- They will never have to move again.
- They will carry the name of God, and the name of the New Jerusalem when it comes down to this earth after the millennium.
- They will also carry God's new name. What will that be? Nobody knows, but it will surely be special.

"Whoever has ears, let them hear what the Spirit says to the churches." So ends the message to Philadelphia.

Revelation 3:14-22: To the Angel of the Church in Laodicea, Write:

14 These are the words of the Amen, the faithful and true witness, the ruler of God's creation.

15 I know your deeds, that you are neither cold nor hot.

> *I wish you were either one or the other!*
>
> *16 So, because you are lukewarm—neither hot nor cold—I am about to spit you out of my mouth.*
>
> *17 You say, 'I am rich; I have acquired wealth and do not need a thing.' But you do not realize that you are wretched, pitiful, poor, blind and naked.*
>
> *18 I counsel you to buy from me gold refined in the fire, so you can become rich; and white clothes to wear, so you can cover your shameful nakedness; and salve to put on your eyes, so you can see.*
>
> *19 Those whom I love I rebuke and discipline. So be earnest and repent.*
>
> *20 Here I am! I stand at the door and knock. If anyone hears my voice and opens the door, I will come in and eat with that person, and they with me.*
>
> *21 To the one who is victorious, I will give the right to sit with me on my throne, just as I was victorious and sat down with my Father on his throne.*
>
> *22 Whoever has ears, let them hear what the Spirit says to the churches.*

This description of Jesus for the last church may have hints about the end of time on this earth. In that case, it could especially be a message for us as well. Amen is what we say at the end of a prayer because we believe and accept the words that were said. In the Old Testament the Israelites said Amen, showing that they agreed with and accepted their covenant with God.

Because Jesus is the faithful and true witness, we can be confident of His help when He uses us as witnesses to His truth.

"The ruler of God's creation" points us back to Genesis 1 and 2. Jesus was the Creator and He put Adam and Eve in charge of the creation. When they sinned, Satan claimed that he was the ruler of this world. But at the end, it will be Jesus who everyone will be happy to have as the ruler of all God's creation.

Unfortunately, God does not have any affirmation for Laodicea. His diagnosis is that they are not whole-heartedly Christian. They say they are Christians, but their words and behavior do not match. God identifies three different groups. He would rather have them either hot—totally on His side—or cold—antagonistic toward Him, rather than spiritually lukewarm, which is basically indifferent. The Laodiceans are the opposite of what they think they are. They think they are rich and prosperous and well-dressed. God sees them in a hugely different way.

His counsel is for them to buy three things from Him:

- **refined gold to make them rich**
- **white clothes to cover their nakedness**
- **eye salve so they could see clearly**

Buying from God doesn't cost any money. He freely gives us everything we need. But it means we accept his diagnosis and agree to follow His counsel.

According to 1 Peter 1:7, gold represents saving faith that would put the Laodiceans totally onto God's side. White clothes would cover them with Christ's righteousness. Eye salve, as bought from God, would give them good eyesight to understand their true condition.

In verse Revelation 3:19, God assures them it is because He loves them that He is giving this counsel. If He did not care about them, He would not bother to take time to give them counsel. He is eagerly waiting to be close friends with them. But in order to enjoy that friendship, they need to stop being half-hearted and experience the joy of total dependence on Jesus for salvation.

The wonderful promise for Laodicea is that when they are victorious, they will sit with Jesus on His throne. It can't get any better than that!

Once again, the message ends with, "Whoever has ears, let them hear what the Spirit says to the churches."

And that brings us to the end of the messages to the seven churches, and to the end of Part 1. Now we continue to chapter 4 and find ourselves watching what is happening in the throne room of the universe.

Symbols in Chapter Three:

- **Soiled clothes, or dressed in white:** symbolize people slipping into sinful ways rather than being totally on God's side, or allowing Him to cover them with His white robe of righteousness

- **Open door:** symbolizes God's invitation to understand what is going on in heaven, and to participate in His mission

- **Key of David:** David was the king of Israel, an ancestor of Jesus. The one with the key controls access. Revelation 3:7 promises that Jesus is the one who controls access to heaven, not any human beings.

- **The hour of trial:** refers to the time of trouble just before Jesus returns to take His people home to heaven

- **Hot:** symbolizes on fire for God, totally committed to Him

- **Cold:** symbolizes a person who is antagonistic toward God

- **Lukewarm:** literally unusable or barren, a self-righteous and self-sufficient person who does not acknowledge or recognize any dependence on God.

- **Refined gold:** symbolizes true spiritual wealth

- **White clothes:** symbolize Jesus' righteousness that covers us

- **Eye salve:** symbolizes wisdom from God so a person can clearly understand the difference between right and wrong

PART II
REVELATION
4 THROUGH 7

> **Revelation 4:1** "After this I looked, and there before me was a door standing open in heaven. And the voice I had first heard speaking to me like a trumpet said, "Come up here, and I will show you what must take place after this."

As John's vision continued, he heard the same voice calling to him like a trumpet, this time telling him to come up. This marks a big change from the messages to the communities of believers.

Remember that the presence of God was in the Most Holy Place of the tent sanctuary that was built at Mt. Sinai. From there He gave directions to His people. Years later, when King Solomon built a new temple, God's presence again entered into the Most Holy Place, communicating from there to His people what they should do.

At the beginning of this vision, Jesus was in the sanctuary on earth, among his people, caring for each group. Now John is called to look at what is happening up in the sanctuary of heaven.

Pay attention to the fact that the door is open. If something this important were happening here on earth, maybe you would only be allowed to observe if you had a special invitation. But God has an open-door policy. Anyone may enter and learn what is taking place. God wants us to know what is going on.

In this part of the vision, we will find to our surprise that there is a big problem in heaven. It has to do with a scroll that is sealed with seven seals. Then the shocking solution will be presented, and the scrolls will begin to be opened one by one.

CHAPTER 4
IN THE THRONE ROOM OF THE UNIVERSE

1 After this I looked, and there before me was a door standing open in heaven. And the voice I had first heard speaking to me like a trumpet said, "Come up here, and I will show you what must take place after this.

2 At once I was in the Spirit, and there before me was a throne in heaven with someone sitting on it.

We have come to an extremely important part of the vision given to John. From here on throughout the rest of the book, the progress of the vision will be in relation to this sanctuary scene in heaven. John will be there watching what is happening throughout the cosmic conflict, and we will be watching over his shoulder.

Jesus Wins! 33

John looks through the open door into the open room and sees that it is a very busy place. We will find that everyone is participating.

John sees:

- A throne with Someone sitting on it who looked like jasper and rubies. These are very beautiful stones. Jasper is usually shades of red, but it can be green or yellow. Rubies come in gorgeous shades of dark pink and are expensive.
- A rainbow that shone like an emerald around the throne. Emeralds are shades of green and also are very expensive.
- Twenty-four more thrones around the throne with twenty-four elders sitting on them. They were dressed in white and had gold crowns on their heads.
- Seven lamps were blazing in front of the throne.
- A sea of glass, clear as crystal, in front of the throne.
- Four living creatures in the center around the throne. Each one had six wings and was covered with eyes.
    - » The first one was like a lion
    - » The second one was like an ox
    - » The third had a face like a man
    - » The fourth was like a flying eagle

Day and night they were all praising God.

The first throne John saw, surrounded with the rainbow, was the throne of God. But why were there twenty-four more thrones? On this earth we would never expect to see a king letting other people sit on thrones around him. Obviously, God is willing to share His power or His responsibility.

Lots of people have tried to discover who these twenty-four elders were. Because of what we will learn as we continue to study, probably these elders were representatives from this earth. If that is true, maybe we know who three of them were: Elijah, Moses and Enoch. The rest could have been the people who were resurrected at the same time as Jesus and went back to heaven with Him.[13] On the other hand, it is possible that they are representatives from other worlds throughout space who have all stayed loyal to God. Maybe some are from earth, and some are from other planets.

---

[13] *Psalm 68:18; Matthew 27:50-53; Ephesians 4:8*

They are all representatives from the place where they have lived.

The Greek word for lamp is different from the word for lampstands in chapter 1, so it means something different. These seven blazing lamps were the seven Spirits of God. This is a symbol for the fulness of the Holy Spirit. Remember the symbolic meaning of the number seven.

The angels with six wings who surround God's throne are called seraphim.[14] John saw that day and night they never stopped saying, "Holy, Holy, Holy." That may sound very boring to you. But remember exaggeration and symbols.

Later in the book we are going to find something else related to this. Revelation 12 tells the big story of the Great Controversy, and in verse 10 you can read that the dragon accuses God's people day and night. So, without ceasing, the battle between Christ and Satan goes on. God's side constantly cheers for Him, and the dragon constantly accuses God's people and works to stir up chaos and trouble.

Whenever the seraphim praise God, the twenty-four elders bow down, put their crowns at God's feet and worship Him as the Creator.

This completes chapter 4. But we will continue to find this huge council mentioned throughout the book. This is the background to what will be revealed throughout John's vision.

Now we will read what John wrote about in chapter 5. To his surprise, and probably to ours, he saw that something was wrong. There was a big problem. How could anything possibly go wrong in a perfect heaven?

---

[14] *Isaiah 6:1-3*

CHAPTER 5
A BIG PROBLEM IN HEAVEN

Revelation 5:1-5:

> *1 Then I saw in the right hand of him who sat on the throne a scroll with writing on both sides and sealed with seven seals.*

God is holding in his right hand a scroll that is sealed with seven seals. Before books were written with pages like we have now, they were written on rolled up lengths of sheep skin or papyrus. It was common for scrolls to be sealed with a few drips of warm wax, then to have the impression of a ring pressed into that. When the wax was cold, it was hard. The impression from the ring showed who had sealed it. Nobody but the correct person was supposed to break the seal and open the scroll.

We think of heaven as a peaceful, happy, perfect place. But if we put together everything we know about sin, we realize that sin we experience on this earth started in heaven long ago. More information will come later on that.

Verses two and three reveal what problem the participants are facing in the throne room.

> *2 And I saw a mighty angel proclaiming in a loud voice, "Who is worthy to break the seals and open the scroll?" But no one in heaven or on earth or under the earth could open the scroll or even look inside it.*

Does this seem a little strange? It is surely easy enough to break that little bit of wax. But the question was, "Who is worthy?" So, that tells us the problem is not about the ability to break the seal, but to find the right person who is supposed to break the seal and reveal what is inside. And the message shows that heaven and earth and beyond had not yet identified the worthy person.

John's reaction to this proclamation by the mighty angel shows just how critical the problem was. He writes that he wept and wept.

"Then one of the elders said to me, "Do not weep! See, the Lion of the tribe of Judah, the Root of David, has triumphed. He is able to open the scroll and its seven seals."

Oh good, the worthy One is a Lion. He is Jesus, the relative of King David. The tribe of Judah provided all the kings of the Jews except for Saul. The Lion has triumphed. That could be translated, "He has won the war." So, He is very strong and well able to reveal what is in the scroll.

When John looks again, instead of a Lion—surprise!—he sees a Lamb that had been killed with violence. But there He is, on the throne of God with the seraphim and the elders around Him.

The Lamb had seven horns and seven eyes—complete perfection again. Horns are symbols for power; eyes are symbols for knowledge and wisdom. Verse 6 says these seven eyes are the seven Spirits of God sent out into all the earth. This is the Holy Spirit, or the Comforter, that Jesus promised He would send to His disciples on earth. Jesus and the Holy Spirit are very closely related.

The Holy Spirit can be everywhere at the same time. Jesus who took human nature upon Himself seems to be limited to one place at a time. When we get to heaven, we can learn more about these things.

The Lamb went and took the scroll from the hand of God. At that moment the four living creatures and the twenty-four elders fell down and worshiped Him. They each had a harp and were holding bowls of incense. Here is another symbol, and verse 8 immediately tells what it means. Incense is the prayers of God's people. Thus, God's praying people were joining in the worship of the Lamb.

Verse nine gives the new song they sang in honor and praise of the Lamb. Since it had never been sung before, probably this was the first time Jesus came into the throne room after He was resurrected and welcomed back to heaven.

The reason they were singing and worshiping was because the Lamb had been slain. By being willing to die for sinners, He had purchased for God every person on the earth, at all times, who chooses to be on God's side. This made Him worthy to open the scroll with seven seals.

The second verse of the new song told that the Lamb had wonderful plans for those people who follow Him. Notice that this is almost the same as John's praise in Revelation 1:6.

- **They would be a kingdom**[15]
- **They would serve God as priests**
- **They will reign on the earth**

Suddenly a massive choir joined the song of praise. Verse eleven says there were millions of angels singing that the Lamb who was slain was worthy. On the last stanza, every bit of God's creation joined in the song of praise to God and the Lamb.

In verse fourteen, the four living creatures said, "Amen," and the elders fell down and worshiped again.

So, God is praised because He allowed the Lamb to be slain. Does that make sense? At least it is very hard to understand. Because God is all powerful, surely He could have solved the problem in an easier way. We will have to stay tuned and see what happens later that will help us to understand this.

---

[15] *Compare Daniel 7:18,22,27*

Now we will turn to chapter six as the Lamb begins to break a seal and open the scroll. We will begin to understand that God's solution to the crisis of the sealed scroll in heaven was revelation, revealing what is behind the curtain, or taking off the lid to show what was hidden in the box.

Symbols in Chapter Five

- **Horns**—symbolize power
- **Eyes**—symbolize knowledge and wisdom
- **Incense**—symbolizes the prayers of God's people

(For additional information about symbols in chapter 4 and 5, see the Symbols in Chapter Six below.)

CHAPTER

6 SIX SEALS

Revelation 6:1-2: Opening the First Seal

> *1 I watched as the Lamb opened the first of the seven seals. Then I heard one of the four living creatures say in a voice like thunder, 'Come!'*
>
> *2 I looked, and there before me was a white horse! Its rider held a bow, and he was given a crown, and he rode out as a conqueror bent on conquest.*

The First Seal begins with a white horse, but we cannot think of the white horse all by itself. It is always part of a set of four horses. Those are seals one, two, three and four. We will find that seals two, three and four are clearly very bad. Is it possible that the first horse is good, if all the other horses in the set represent something bad? We need to look very carefully at the white horse and its rider for clues about their character.

Before we think about the horse, let's pay attention to the fact that one of the four living creatures from around the throne takes part. In a very loud voice, he says "Come!" as if he might be saying, "Come out and show yourself!" Clearly the opening of this seal continues to be part of the heavenly council scene in heaven.

Many people have thought that because the horse was white, that meant it and its rider were good. But the white horse is tightly connected to the other three colored horses. So, let's see what clues we can find.

The rider is carrying a bow. What can that tell us? We don't find any stories about Jesus carrying a bow. He has that double-edged sword in his mouth that symbolizes truthful witness. Neither is a bow included in the full armor of God (Ephesians 6:10-17). Can we find any Bible story about a bow? Yes, in Ezekiel 38 and 39 there is a long prophecy about enemies of God's people in the last days. Gog is their leader. In Ezekiel 39:3 we read that when God destroys the enemies in order to protect His people, Gog will lose his bow and arrows. Then God's people will gather up all the weapons, including the bows and arrows and have enough wood to burn for seven years (Ezekiel 39:9).

Let's look at two other aspects of this rider. Revelation 6:2, NIV, says that the rider of the white horse was given a crown. Who gave him his crown? We will return to this question later. Second, he rode out as a conqueror bent on conquest. If you are bent on winning a race at your school, can you be positive that you will win? You are determined to win, but it remains to be seen what will happen. The rider saw himself as a conqueror, but was he really going to conquer?

Now let's compare what John heard about Jesus. We have to re-read Revelation 5:4-5. John was weeping and weeping because he was so upset about the crisis he saw taking place in heaven. Then one of the elders told him not to weep because Jesus had triumphed. Jesus had already won, and that made Him worthy to open the seals on the scroll. So, Jesus had already been triumphant, He had already won. But the rider of the white horse is determined to win. That means Jesus and the rider of the white horse may not represent the same type of character. Possibly the white horse has been stolen by someone who wants to pretend to be like Jesus. We will return to this possibility after we cover the next three seals.

Revelation 6:3-8: Opening the Second, Third and Fourth Seals

> 3 When the Lamb opened the second seal, I heard the second living creature say, "Come!"
>
> 4 Then another horse came out, a fiery red one. Its rider was given power to take peace from the earth and to make people kill each other. To him was given a large sword.
>
> 5 When the Lamb opened the third seal, I heard the third living creature say, "Come!" I looked, and there before me was a black horse! Its rider was holding a pair of scales in his hand.
>
> 6 Then I heard what sounded like a voice among the four living creatures, saying, "Two pounds of wheat for a day's wages, and six pounds of barley for a day's wages, and do not damage the oil and the wine!"
>
> 7 When the Lamb opened the fourth seal, I heard the voice of the fourth living creature say, "Come!"
>
> 8. I looked, and there before me was a pale horse! Its rider was named Death, and Hades was following close behind him. They were given power over a fourth of the earth to kill by sword, famine and plague, and by the wild beasts of the earth.

When the Lamb opened the Second Seal, another one of the four creatures around the throne called out, "Come!" A fiery red horse came charging out. Its rider was given power to take away peace and to make people kill each other. and he was given a large sword. This was not a double-edged sword which represented truth, this was a weapon for killing. This rider and his red horse represent war in the world.

When the Lamb opened the Third Seal, the third member of the living creatures around the throne said, "Come!" Instantly John saw before him a black horse! Its rider was holding a pair of scales. Someone close to the throne of God announced its meaning. A day's wages would only buy two pounds of wheat or 6 pounds of barley. That means there was famine. A family could not live on only two pounds of wheat. They could do a little better on six pounds of barley, but barley was not as desirable as wheat. The voice continued with a restriction. There was no permission to damage the oil or the wine. This rider and his black horse symbolize famine in the world.

When the Lamb opened the Fourth Seal, the last of the four living creatures called out, "Come!" And there in front of John was a pale yellowish-grey horse. That color is the ashen appearance of a dead body. And the rider was named Death. He was followed closely by Hades which is hell or the grave. The two of them were given power over a quarter of the people on earth to kill by sword, famine, pestilence and by wild beasts. This is a sort of summary of the other bad things that happened under the previous seals.

Traditionally we have thought of these seals as a historical sequence of what happened during the years between John's vision and the Second Coming of Jesus. In some ways that can be true, but not in all ways. There has been murder and war ever since Cain killed Abel and all the years since then. The earth was filled with violence before Noah's flood. Famine has struck the earth many times. In the Old Testament we find Abraham and Jacob going to Egypt because there was famine in the land. Naomi and her family moved to Moab because of famine. There was widespread famine during the three and a half years when Elijah predicted no rain.

What are the seals revealing? There is nothing new about the bad things that were permitted under the seals we have read about. Certainly, war and famine and death have continued all the years between John's vision and now. But they had also happened almost all the years since the Garden of Eden. So, what is so mysterious about the unsealing of the scroll?

Now it is time to think back to the First Seal. What could that Seal be revealing to us? Many people have seen similarities between the Seals and Jesus' predictions about the end of time in Matthew 24 and Luke 21. Let's look at that. Both start out with a warning about being deceived. Then follows war and famine. Luke includes pestilences, and we will see that all three include injustice in the form of persecution.

	Revelation 6		Matthew 24		Luke 21	
First Seal	Verses 1,2	?????	Verses 4,5	Deception	Verse 8	Deception
Second Seal	Verses 3,4	War	Verses 6,7	War	Verses 9,10	War
Third Seal	Verses 5,6	Famine	Verses 7,8	Famine	Verse 11	Famine & Pestilences
Fourth Seal	Verses 7,8	Death	Verse 9	Death	Verse 16	Death

When you see the comparison among these three Bible passages, I believe it will raise your suspicions even higher that the First Seal is revealing deception. Somebody is trying to pass himself off as somebody else. The riders on the red, black and sickly grey horse clearly symbolize demonic activity. What about the rider on the white horse?

What Jesus is revealing to us is not just history, although history does somewhat follow this pattern, but Jesus is revealing to us what the demonic side is doing to mankind and the earth. In each case you see that the horse and rider are allowed to do certain things. But they are also held under some kind of restraint.

The first rider was given a crown. He went out determined to win the war. The second rider was given a large sword and power to cause people to kill each other. The third rider carried a pair of scales, but he was not allowed to damage the oil or the wine. The fourth rider, along with the grave or hell, was given power to kill a fourth part of the earth, but the other three fourths, apparently, he couldn't touch.

I believe we can tentatively suggest that what Jesus is revealing is the reality of deception, war, famine and death and disease caused by demonic powers. Jesus surely is not causing those; He is revealing or exposing them. God allows certain things to happen, but He restrains demonic powers from doing other things.

Because we are re-readers, we can find plenty of evidence throughout the Bible that Satan is a master deceiver. In the Garden of Eden, he deceived Eve. Satan's character is deceitful, devious, and cunning as in every way possible he seeks to influence or force people to be on his side. Let's just look at some of the evidence.

Genesis 3:13 – Eve says that the serpent deceived her.

Rev 2:9 – He leads his followers to slander God's people, telling lies about their characters and their activities. And that started in heaven when Satan deceived a third of the angels by slandering Jesus and God and turning the angels away from them. (Revelation 12:4)

Rev 3:9 – He causes his followers to lie about the people of God. He will do anything to try and get people to choose his side in the battle that is going on. Remember, he is determined to win the war. (Revelation 6:2; Isaiah 14:12-14)

Rev 12:9 – He leads the whole world astray, in fact, he had success in heaven leading angels astray. This is more than a battle just here on earth. This is a cosmic battle that involves the whole universe! It is not a battle of guns and ammunition; it is a war of words. Our responsibility is to determine which side is telling the truth.

Revelation 12 – Right in the middle of John's vision, the story of the huge battle is summarized. The great dragon, the serpent, is called the devil, or Satan. He deceives the whole world.

Rev 13:13-14 – In chapter 13 we find him directing the actions of deceptive people in their efforts to force God's people to follow them or be killed. Even false miracles will be performed to convince people that Satan's side is the correct one, not based on truth, but based on force and power.

What is Satan's purpose in all the deception and slander and lies and violence? He wants to be worshipped! He is trying desperately to receive the worship that belongs only to God. Remember when he tempted Jesus in the wilderness, the third temptation was an offer to give the kingdoms of the earth to Jesus if He would just bow down and worship him.[16] Isaiah 14:12-14 revealed what Satan's ambition was. And in Revelation 13:4 he

---

[16] *Matthew 4:8, 9*

succeeds in persuading or forcing everyone in the world to worship him unless they are totally committed to Jesus.

> **Rev 20:2, 3,10** – There finally comes a time when Satan is no longer able to deceive anyone. That is because all God's people will have been taken to heaven, and all those who did not decide to be on God's side will be dead. Satan will be imprisoned on this empty earth for a thousand years, left alone with no one to deceive. If your parents have ever given you a timeout, you understand how hard it can be to be left alone with nothing but your thoughts. Imagine that for a thousand years!

Then verse 3 ends by saying that after that he must be set free for a short time. Why? When the thousand years is ended, for what purpose will he be set free? Fast forward to verses 7 and 8. He will not have learned anything from his timeout. He will be deceiving the nations again and leading them in trying to overthrow God and His people so he and his followers can occupy the beautiful New Jerusalem.

From beginning to end, Satan is a deceiver with nothing on his mind but determination to win the war and receive worship that belongs only to God.

Let's go back to Revelation chapter five to understand more about what is taking place.

> *Revelation 5:6 Then I saw a Lamb, looking as if it had been slain,* **standing at the center of the throne, encircled by the four living creatures and the elders.**
>
> **9 And they sang a new song, saying:**
> *"You are worthy to take the scroll*
> *and to open its seals,*
> *because you were slain,*
> **and with your blood you purchased for God persons from every tribe and language and people and nation."**
>
> **11 Then I looked and heard the voice of many angels, numbering thousands upon thousands, and ten thousand times ten thousand. They encircled the throne and the living creatures and the elders.**

> **12 In a loud voice they were saying:**
> *"Worthy is the Lamb, who was slain,*
> **to receive power and wealth and wisdom and strength and honor and glory and praise!"**
> **(emphasis supplied)**

There was a crisis in heaven over finding someone who could open the scroll. It seems like any problem in heaven should be easy to fix. And yet this was an unfixable problem until the slain Lamb was identified. We know that, for John wept and wept because no one in heaven or on earth or under the earth could open the scroll or even look inside it (Revelation 5:3, 4). The huge council in heaven was faced with something that was mysterious even to them. They knew what was happening on the earth right then. That was what concerned them, not the future they did not know. Then Jesus was identified, and it was He Himself, because He was slain, who was the solution to the problem. They were perplexed because of what God was allowing to happen.

In Ezekiel 2:9, 10 we read about another scroll. It was similarly written on the front and the back, and the contents were known. It had words of lament and mourning and woe, just like the scroll that Jesus was unsealing in Revelation 6.

We already know that what would be revealed was nothing new to humanity. Instead, it was the reality of life on this sinful earth. The four living creatures from around the throne were participating in the revelation, so it seems that they knew about the content. The revelation is about something we would never think of, or could not imagine, if we were not shown. There is something here we need to comprehend. Maybe it is something we need to understand in a new way. Maybe we need to change our minds about how we understand the meaning of what was happening here. We need to understand why the world is the way it is.

Before we leave the horses and riders, it is important to look at who it is who gives them something or takes something from them. The first rider was given a crown, The second rider was given power to take away peace and to make people kill each other, and he was given a sword. The third rider was allowed to bring famine but not allowed to damage the oil and the wine. The fourth rider and the grave or hell following him were given power to kill one fourth of the people on earth. What is this all about? How is this related to the revealing that Jesus, the Lamb that was slain, is giving?

In the Old Testament God takes responsibility for everything that happens. He takes the blame for it. Then, after much of the Old Testament had already been written, Isaiah 14:12-15 and Ezekiel 28:12-19 give information about Satan, and it begins to be very clear that God is not the only one working in the world.

But add up all the Old Testament passages about not worshipping other gods, and you begin to see that the Old Testament includes a great deal about Satan although he was in the background and not yet named. If the people were not faithfully worshipping God, who were they worshipping? Those gods might be going by the name of Baal or Ashtoreth or Moloch or Chemosh or Ashur or Marduk or Nabu, but who was behind all of them? The majority of the population was following a culture totally different from the happy peaceful good way God wished them to live. By following gods instead of God, they were making it impossible for God to give them all the blessings He had in store for them.

The New Testament gives much more information about Satan. But God is so much stronger. Why doesn't He just stop Satan? Job was perplexed about what God allowed to happen to him.[17] Habakkuk was concerned because God was not doing what he thought He should do.[18] And here we find the heavenly council silent in the face of things going on that they thought should not be allowed. Why didn't God fix the problem? God takes responsibility for giving the first rider the crown, the second rider the power to cause fighting and war, the third rider to cause famine and the fourth rider together with the grave or hell to kill one fourth of the people on earth.

God is involved in a war of words with Satan who has accused God of being unjust, selfish, arbitrary, unforgiving, and severe. God had the task of convincing the entire universe that Satan was wrong. When Jesus came to this earth to show the universe what God is really like, He revealed by His life and by His death that Satan has lied. God is the same unselfish, loving and caring person that people saw in Jesus. For thousands of years this war has been going on. While being fair even with Satan, God continues to demonstrate His love for each human and creature on earth.

In the vision given to John, Jesus reveals the reality of what the other side is doing. Life on this earth is like it is because Satan claims to be the prince of this world. God still ultimately controls what happens. He gives and takes away according to what He sees as best in the long run. Jesus has

---

[17] *Job 3*
[18] *Habakkuk 1:2-3*

already won the war, but the battle continues in each heart until everyone finally makes up their mind about which side to join.

Jesus' unimaginable revelation pulls aside the curtain to allow us to see what happens in the war between God and Satan. God fights by way of truthful words in the Bible and by giving each individual freedom of choice. Satan uses deception and force to deceive the world into thinking that he is too powerful to resist. He uses entertainment and influence and riches to make people think his side is better. We have the choice of deciding who we want to believe. In each of the seals we see evil satanic actions revealed by Jesus the slain Lamb but allowed and controlled by God.

Now we will turn our attention to the opening of the Fifth Seal.

Revelation 6:9-11: The Fifth Seal

> *9 When he opened the fifth seal, I saw under the altar the souls of those who had been slain because of the word of God and the testimony they had maintained.*
>
> *10 They called out in a loud voice, "How long, Sovereign Lord, holy and true, until you judge the inhabitants of the earth and avenge our blood?"*
>
> *11 Then each of them was given a white robe, and they were told to wait a little longer, until the full number of their fellow servants, their brothers and sisters, were killed just as they had been.*

Each of the first four seals is announced by one of the four living creatures thundering, "Come!" Now that we reach the fifth seal it is different. The focus is still on satanic action, but this time the action is specifically against God's people who have been killed. They are shown as a metaphor for injustice as their shed blood cries to God for vindication. The reality is different from what was expected to happen. Like the participants in the heavenly council, they symbolically wonder why God isn't doing something about the evil that is taking place.

Remember the first martyr in Genesis 4:10. God told Cain that Abel's blood was crying out to Him from the ground. None of the martyrs has really cried to God for justice. They are dead and waiting peacefully for the resurrection. But the righteous who are living know what happened to them and have questions for God. How could You let this happen? What are You going to do about this? How long will this continue to go on? Why didn't You protect Your people? Why do bad things happen to good people?

Especially the question, "How long?" has a lengthy echo in the Old Testament. If you want evidence of that, you can read the following texts:

> **Psalm 6:3; 74:9,10; 79:5; 80:4; 90:13; 94:3-7**
> **Job 7:19**
> **Isaiah 6:11**
> **Jeremiah 4:21; 23:26; 47:5,6**
> **Daniel 8:13; 12:6**
> **Habakkuk 1:2-4**
> **Zechariah 1:12**

We can only deal with any of these questions by first of all understanding the cosmic battle going on between God and Satan, and secondly, by trusting, like Abraham did, that the Judge of all the earth will do right (Genesis 18:25).

Now we can add to the chart.

	Revelation 6		**Matthew 24 & Luke 21**	
First Seal	Verses 1, 2	Deception	Verses 4,5,24-26	Deception
Second Seal	Verses 3, 4	War	Verses 6, 7	War
Third Seal	Verses 5, 6	Famine	Verses 7, 8	Famine
Fourth Seal	Verses 7,8	Pestilence	Luke 21:10	Pestilence
Fifth Seal	Verses 9-11	Injustice	Matthew 24 9	Injustice

Revelation 6:11 is a symbolic picture of God's care for the martyrs. He pays attention to the concerns of His people. They are given white robes which are a symbol of the righteousness of Christ assuring them of eternal life. And they are told to wait a little longer. We have to be patient and long-suffering as we wait for the end of the war. God truthfully admits that other of His people will also be killed for their faith before the end of time.

We don't want to make the same mistake the children of Israel made in the wilderness. "But they soon forgot what He had done and did not wait for His plan to unfold." Psalm 106:13 NIV.

Here in Revelation, we are learning about His plan. In chapter 13:10 we will read that, "This calls for patient endurance and faithfulness on the part of God's people." And in chapter 14:12, again we will find that, "This calls for patient endurance on the part of the people of God who keep his commands and remain faithful to Jesus."

It is hard to wait and be patient, but the final rewards for doing that are stupendous: eternal life with Jesus our elder Brother and the Creator of the universe, as well as our family and friends and pets from our time here on this sinful earth; the opportunity to visit with the angels who helped us and hear the stories of those we have read about in the Bible. There will be endless time in a perfect world for fellowship and space travel and learning and building and creativity and fun.

All those who die for Christ's sake will be fully satisfied that God's justice and judgment did the right thing, and that they have been totally vindicated for their sacrifice.

Review of the First Five Seals

White Horse	Red Horse	Black Horse	Sickly Horse	Martyrs
DECEPTION	WAR	FAMINE	DEATH	INJUSTICE
Demonic	Demonic	Demonic	Demonic	Demonic
(Satan acts)	(Satan acts)	(Satan acts)	(Satan acts)	(Satan acts)
(God permits)	(God permits)	(God permits)	(God permits)	(God permits)
(Jesus reveals)	(Jesus reveals)	(Jesus reveals)	(Jesus reveals)	(Jesus reveals)

Revelation 6:12-17 and Revelation 8:1: The Sixth and Seventh Seals

12 I watched as he opened the sixth seal. There was a great earthquake. The sun turned black like sackcloth made of goat hair, the whole moon turned blood red,

13 and the stars in the sky fell to earth, as figs drop from a fig tree when shaken by a strong wind.

14 The heavens receded like a scroll being rolled up, and every mountain and island was removed from its place.

15 Then the kings of the earth, the princes, the generals, the rich, the mighty, and everyone else, both slave and free, hid in caves and among the rocks of the mountains.

16 They called to the mountains and the rocks, "Fall on us and hide us from the face of him who sits on the throne and from the wrath of the Lamb!

17 For the great day of their wrath has come, and who can withstand it?"

Revelation 8:1 When he opened the seventh seal, there was silence in heaven for about half an hour.

When Jesus the slain Lamb removed the sixth seal from the scroll another huge change takes place. It seems as though everything on the earth and in the sky is falling apart. This is cosmic disorder on an unimaginable scale. What in the world is going on?

You probably know the story of Queen Esther. If you don't, it might be worth your while to read those few chapters. In the early chapters it seems like everything is okay, provided you are willing to accept beauty pageants that include a sleep-over. Then the wicked Haman is introduced and the Jews face extermination. A modern example is Auschwitz and all the other camps when the Nazis intended to kill all the Jews in Europe. Humanly speaking there was no possibility of escape. Haman could sit down to drink with the king then go home to brag to his family about his power and influence and riches and many sons. Then, suddenly, at one point in the story, it turns out Haman does not have all the power on his side. From there on, all the power is on the side of God's people.

The same thing happens in the seven seals. The first four seals all reveal the terrible things happening on earth which Satan and his side are allowed to cause. It doesn't appear that God is doing anything to help. Then there comes a point when it is clear that God is in full control of working out His plan. First, in the fifth seal, He reveals His care for His people who have suffered for him. Then, when Jesus opens the sixth seal the earth and the sky are falling apart. An earthquake, the sun the moon the stars, the heavens receding like a scroll being rolled up, every mountain and island being removed from its place! Those are all terrifying things happening. The whole package plan was clearly not being orchestrated by Satan. Everyone on his side, instead of proudly strutting around, arrogantly persecuting God's people, are suddenly terrified and willing to do anything to escape from the power of God.

Their terror is like that of King Belshazzar who was self-importantly boasting about the power of his gods over the God of heaven one minute, then after seeing the handwriting on the wall is reduced to fear so great that his face was pale, his legs became weak, and his knees were knocking together.[19]

When God chooses to make His presence known, the natural world participates. Every person pays attention and recognizes His sovereignty. There are no exceptions. Do we have other examples of that in the Old Testament?

Elijah was hiding in a cave to protect himself from Jezebel. Then he received instruction from God (1 Kings 19:11). The Lord was about to pass by. There came a terrific destructive wind, next a monumental earthquake, and finally a raging fire. Elijah came out of the cave and God spoke to him in a gentle whisper.

Even when Moses asked to see God's glory he was protected in a cleft of a rock while God passed by (Exodus 33:18–23).

Mt. Sinai is the ultimate example. Exodus 19:16-18 and Exodus 20:18, 19 describe the thunder, lightning, dark cloud, deafening trumpet blast, fire and smoke, and the whole mountain violently trembling. Everyone but Moses was terrified.

In the heavenly council the four beasts, the twenty-one elders, and the millions of angels all loved and trusted their divine leaders, but they had questions about what was happening on earth. That caused the crisis in heaven. Gathered around the throne of God they were silent in the face of the question, "Who is worthy to break the seals and open the scroll?"

Then it was revealed that the Lamb who had been slain with violence was the one who was worthy. He was the solution to the crisis in heaven. All the participants watched as Jesus opened the seals one by one. Slowly

---

[19] *Daniel 5:5-6*

they came to a recognition of God's plan. As the sixth seal was opened and the cosmic turmoil took place, their comprehension became complete.

When the final seal is removed from the scroll, their reaction to God's perfect plan to maintain both his law and the freedom of choice for each individual is revealed. There is silence in heaven for half an hour. They are speechless in the presence of this revelation. In Isaiah 52:13-15 there is a prediction of speechless silence among the kings of many nations as they see Jesus in His power and glory after He had been violently slain and so disfigured that He hardly looked human.

So, the silence in heaven is explained by a revelation in progress. A revelation even more spectacular than that at Mt. Sinai. In the Sixth Seal, God was about to appear, to speak, to show Himself. Anyone not on His side could not survive such an appearance.

Symbols in Chapter Six

- **A white horse:** White is usually a positive symbol of victory and purity, but all the evidence must be considered in this case.
- **A Bow:** represents a weapon of conquest
- **A Crown:** a symbol of rulership. He was "bent on conquest." He intended to win, but that remains to be seen.
- **The red horse:** represents war by the color of blood
- **A large sword:** in this case represents a weapon for killing
- **The black horse:** the negative color represents mourning and sorrow and famine
- **A pair of scales:** represents how much food a day's wages will buy. One person would eat about two pounds of food in a day, so the wages were only enough to buy wheat for one person, or the less desirable barley for three people.
- **Oil and Wine:** These were two other valuable crops in the Bible lands at the time. The olive trees and grape vines had deeper roots than the grain so they could survive the time of famine, but the wages were not high enough for

average people to buy them. They can also represent the Holy Spirit and the blessings of God that are always available to those who are on God's side in the war.

- **The color of the fourth horse:** represents disease and death by sword, famine, plague and wild beasts. In Jeremiah 34:17, 20 and Ezekiel 14:21 all four of these are listed as the dangers of being disobedient and unfaithful to God. Those who are faithful to God are the survivors. God is not killing the unfaithful. Rather, their protection is lost by choosing not to follow the good plans that God has put in place, or by choosing idol worship, which is really worshiping Satan.

(The following is a review of the scene in the throne room.)

- **The slain Lamb in the middle of the throne:** is Jesus.
- **The four living creatures:** are four seraphim angels that look like a lion, an ox, a man, and a flying eagle. They each have six wings and are worship leaders standing the closest to the throne of God. They participate in the opening of the seals. Maybe they are representatives for wild animals, domestic animals, and human beings, all created on the sixth day; plus, the eagle representing the birds created on the fifth day. We should continue to think about what their appearance represents. We may have to wait until heaven to find out for sure.
- **The twenty-four elders:** are seated on thrones around the throne of God, showing how willing God is to share his rulership responsibilities. Maybe Enoch and Moses are two of them. Elijah could be one. Others might be the people who were resurrected and ascended together with Jesus when He went back to heaven (Matthew 27:50-53; Isaiah 26:19 KJV). We don't really know who they are. This is something else for us to continue to ponder and find out for sure when we get to heaven. Meanwhile, here is an interesting statement about those who rose with Jesus:

"As Christ arose, He brought from the grave a multitude of captives. The earthquake at His death had rent open their graves, and when He arose, they came forth with Him. They were those who had been co-laborers with God, and who at the cost of their lives had borne testimony to the truth. Now they were to be witnesses for Him who had raised them from the dead." ". . . those who came forth from the grave at Christ's resurrection were raised to everlasting life. They ascended with Him as trophies of His victory over death and the grave." *Desire of Ages*, page. 786

- **The angels who encircled the throne to sing praises to the slain Lamb:** To get an idea of how many angels were there, use your calculator to multiply 1,000 times 1,000, and then 10,000 times 10,000. Add those two big numbers together.

- **The altar:** draws our minds to the sacrificial system in the Old Testament. There were two altars: the altar of sacrifice and the altar of incense. In the Fifth Seal the reference can only be to the altar of sacrifice because it is the one mentioned as having activity at its base (Exodus 29:12; Deuteronomy 12:27). Paul says that he was already being poured out (2 Timothy 4:6), referring to himself as a sacrifice at the altar. The Great Sacrifice was Jesus who died for our sins. All martyrs have shared in Jesus' suffering.

- **Souls of those who had been slain:** the martyrs through the ages who have been killed because they remained faithful to God instead of going along with the majority who followed Satan

- **A white robe:** symbolizes being covered with the righteousness of Christ which guarantees our salvation

- **The full number to be killed:** Millions in the past have been unjustly killed. We can expect to continue to hear about God's people here and there in the world dying for their faith in Jesus. That will no longer happen after probation closes.

- **Monumental upheavals of nature:** symbolize the power of God displayed at the Second Coming of Jesus

- **Reaction of those on Satan's side:** shows that the tables are turned. They thought they were in control, but suddenly they realize they have bet on the wrong horse. Their fear, disappointment and panic are evident. They realize their death is imminent because they cannot survive in the presence of God.

- **The wrath of God:** God is love. He is not willing that any should perish (Matthew 18:14). Yet He does not leave the guilty unpunished (Exodus 34:7). God's wrath does not mean He loses His temper.

If we prefer Satan's lies to the truth, if we persist in rejecting God's every effort to save and heal, there is nothing else he can do but sadly give us up and hand us over to the awful consequence of our own rebellious choice. (See Hosea 11:8 and 12:14 for an example of this.) This is what it means to experience God's wrath unmixed with mercy at the end. God would do anything to spare us from this final destruction. There is no sin He would not be happy to forgive.

CHAPTER 7
INTERMISSION OR INTERVENTION

Revelation 7:1-8: God's People Sealed

> *1 After this I saw four angels standing at the four corners of the earth, holding back the four winds of the earth to prevent any wind from blowing on the land or on the sea or on any tree.*
>
> *2 Then I saw another angel coming up from the east, having the seal of the living God. He called out in a loud voice to the four angels who had been given power to harm the land and the sea:*
>
> *3 "Do not harm the land or the sea or the trees until we put a seal on the foreheads of the servants of our God."*

Before we come to the Seventh Seal, there is something important happening for God's people on earth. Revelation chapter seven has been explained to be an intermission. But it is better to think of it as an intervention of protection going on during the sixth seal, probably near the beginning. The climax of wickedness on earth has come. We read in Revelation 6:15-16 what the wicked were doing. But what led up to that? Here in chapter seven, we read what is happening to God's people during this crisis time. Each one has made a final decision to be on God's side. God puts a seal on each forehead to show that these people belong to Him. A seal on the forehead represents our thinking, decision making and choices. It means that we belong to God, and nothing will ever change that. He is taking care of His people during these final extreme events. In fact, in Revelation 7:1, we read that evil is being restrained.

Because we are re-readers of Revelation, we may be aware of what we will find in chapter 13. At the same time that God is sealing His people, Satan is putting a mark on his people, but there is a difference. That mark can be on their forehead OR on their hand. The forehead shows that they agree with him in their thinking, decision making and choices. The mark on a hand means they just go along with his commands even though they don't really believe in what he says.

Revelation chapter seven is filled with wonderful things in groups of verses revealing what we will go through. First of all, in verses 1-3 that are written above, there are four angels holding back the winds of evil power. Then another angel carrying the seal tells those angels to wait to harm the earth until God's people are sealed. God is restraining the forces of evil. Every time you read one third, think of the two-thirds that are spared. All through the six seals and the six trumpets, the demonic activity is getting increasingly worse. God is constantly putting a cap on what they are allowed to do. He is always protecting and caring for His people. Bad things may happen to us, but no more than God allows.

Verses 4 through 8: Here we read the names of the 12 tribes of Israel who each have 12,000 sealed. It is interesting that the tribe of Dan and one of the sons of Joseph are missing. Apparently, those tribes gave themselves over completely to worshipping idols, which is the same as worshiping Satan.

Many writers have contributed ideas about whether this number is literal or symbolic. Remember that John was told that the vision would be symbolic. The northern ten tribes were lost to history when their territory was overrun by Assyria. God knows who His people are, and here He is showing us that His plan for the family of Israel comes to pass.

Revelation 7:9-17: An Innumerable Multitude In Heaven

Verses 9 and 10: John saw an innumerable multitude in heaven from every part of the earth who were wearing white robes and waving palm branches. In loud voices they cry, "Salvation belongs to our God who sits on the throne and to the Lamb." They recognize that they have only been saved because of the victory of the slain Lamb. Palm branches represent victory. When Jesus was riding on a colt into Jerusalem, crowds were accompanying him with palm branches because they thought He was about to declare Himself king (Matthew 21:7-9; John 12:12,13).

Verses 11 and 12: Millions of angels standing around the throne, and the elders, and the four living creatures all add their voices to the praise of God. Now that they comprehend more of God's plans they are so awe-struck that they fall on their faces before the throne and worship God.

Next, in **verse 13**, one of the elders asks John a question: "Who is this multitude wearing white robes and where did they come from?" John's answer was the same as ours would be if someone asked us the same question.

Verse 14, "Sir, you know."

The rest of chapter seven is the elder's explanation. These people have remained faithful to God throughout the events of their years on earth. No matter what happened to them, they held on to their faith and hope in God. Therefore, this is what God is going to do for them. When you read through these remaining verses, I'm sure you will want to be one of that multitude.

How big do you think the temple in heaven is? Around the throne are the 4 living creatures and the elders and the millions of angels. Now is added the multitude that is so great that no one could count them. Wow! That has to be an enormously huge temple. We construct buildings because we need a cover from the weather, and we need walls for protection. Neither of those conditions apply in heaven. There is no reason why the temple in heaven has to be an actual building. Some of the most beautiful and functional spaces, even on earth, are open-air. The scenery provides the surroundings, rather than walls and roofs. Adam and Eve lived in a garden, not a mansion. The temple in heaven may be a fabulous garden.

CHAPTER 7   Intermission Or Intervention

Well, good! The story is finished. Bad things have happened. God's people have been patient and faithful. Jesus has come the second time. What more can there possibly be to say? Oh dear, wait. We've made a good start, but we have a long way to go.

Symbols in Chapter Seven

- **Winds**: represent evil powers that want to harm the earth and its people but were being restrained by God's angels
- **The number of those who were sealed:** the representatives of God's chosen people. We will understand more about them when we get to heaven. Maybe we will be among that group.
- **Innumerable multitude:** All the saved of all ages are gathered together in heaven.
- **White robes:** the protective covering of Jesus' righteousness. They don't enter heaven because they were good enough. They are there because Jesus lived and died for them, and they have accepted His righteousness in their behalf and lived for Him.

PART III
THE SEVEN TRUMPETS

There is something interesting that we find in the Bible over and over. It is called repetition and enlargement. That means the same events are covered again but are enlarged with additional details. When you read Genesis 1 and then Genesis 2 you see that much of the same story is being told again, but with different features. In Daniel 2, God revealed to the king the history of the world from his day to the end of time. Once that has been shown, the history does not change. But Daniel 7 goes over the same time frame with more points. Daniel 8 again goes over the same time but with different aspects. And so on throughout the book of Daniel. Bible poetry is mostly half a verse stating something, then the next half verse stating the same thing but in a different way. This helps the reader understand better what the verse is talking about. And we can learn from this that God always has something new to teach us.

We have come to the next large segment of Revelation that will seem to cover the same ground as the seven seals, but with very different details. Again, we will need to carefully watch for what it is that Jesus is revealing to John on the island of Patmos.

CHAPTER 8

THE SEVENTH SEAL AND THE FOUR TRUMPETS

Revelation 8:1: Silence in Heaven

Before a discussion of the Seven Trumpets, we find that the person who divided the Bible into chapters put the Seventh Seal into the first verse of Revelation 8.

> *1 When he opened the seventh seal, there was silence in heaven for about half an hour.*

Some commentators have thought that there was silence in heaven because heaven was empty while all the angels are accompanying Jesus down to earth for the Second Coming. And the Seventh Seal does include the Second Coming, but I believe there is another explanation for the silence. On Satan's side we have encountered deception and war and famine and death and injustice. Yet, Jesus wins the war by being the Lamb killed with violence. How can that possibly be? How can that make sense? Let's look to the Old Testament for help in understanding.

Jesus Wins! **65**

Isaiah 52:13-15

> *13 See, my servant will prosper;*
> *he will be raised and lifted up and highly exalted.*
>
> *14 Just as there were many who were appalled at him—his appearance was so disfigured beyond that of any humanbeing and his form marred beyond human likeness—*
>
> *15 so will many nations be amazed at him, and kings will shut their mouths because of him. For what they were not told, they will see, and what they have not heard, they will understand.*

The book of Isaiah has been called the Fifth Gospel because it reveals so much about Jesus, even though it was written about seven hundred years before Jesus was born in Bethlehem.

Isaiah tells us in chapter 52 that Jesus would be greatly exalted even though He had been disfigured and his form marred by crucifixion. This would cause people and even kings of many different nations to be amazed. It was something they hadn't seen or heard, nor could they even imagine it. But when it was finally evident and they understood what had happened, they would be speechless.

In heaven, after six seals have been opened, and the elders and creatures and angels finally understood what God and Jesus are doing about sin, they would be speechless with amazement. They had not expected this. They had not imagined it. They had been perplexed and worried. But now they are overwhelmed as they realize how God is dealing with the problem of sin and suffering. They don't have a word to say. There is silence in heaven for about half an hour.

Revelation 8:2-5: The Golden Censer

> *2 And I saw the seven angels who stand before God, and seven trumpets were given to them.*
>
> *3 Another angel, who had a golden censer, came and stood at the altar. He was given much incense to offer,*

> *with the prayers of all God's people, on the golden altar in front of the throne.*
>
> *4 The smoke of the incense, together with the prayers of God's people, went up before God from the angel's hand.*
>
> *5 Then the angel took the censer, filled it with fire from the altar, and hurled it on the earth; and there came peals of thunder, rumblings, flashes of lightning and an earthquake.*

This beautiful little introduction about the golden censer brings us to the seven trumpets and reminds us that heaven is very involved in everything that is happening on the earth. Seven angels who stand before God are given seven trumpets. Another angel has a golden censer and is given lots of incense to offer with the prayers of God's people at the golden altar. These eight are clearly angels on God's side in the cosmic conflict.

Prayer is an important part of this introduction to the seven trumpets. The other angel was given much incense to offer with the prayers of God's people, so God's people must have been praying a lot. And God was paying attention to those prayers.

You will probably remember that incense was offered on the altar in the first room of the sanctuary, the Holy Place. The coals of fire were carried in a censer by a priest from the altar out in the courtyard and placed on this smaller golden altar. This altar stood in front of the throne because it stood just in front of the veil separating the Holy Place and the Most Holy Place. God's throne was in the Most Holy Place. The incense added to the coals made a sweet-smelling perfume of the smoke that rose above the altar and wafted into the Most Holy place over the veil. The incense symbolized Jesus' righteousness being added to the prayers.

What do we make of the angel throwing down the censer on the earth? There is something similar in Ezekiel 10:2,6,7. There someone is told to take handfuls of coals from under God's throne and scatter them on the earth. No censer is mentioned. The context is God abandoning Jerusalem to captivity by the Babylonians because of their idolatry.

In Early Writings, page 279, there is a clear statement that Jesus throws down the censer when He receives word that the redeemed are sealed. At that moment his intercession for sinners ends and the plagues begin.

It is the ultimate throw-down-the-mic moment for the universe in the cosmic conflict. The same statement, almost word for word, is quoted in four other books. But Jesus throwing down the censer is different from the story in Ezekiel. Here in Revelation 8:5, it is again different. An angel hurls down the censer on the earth and thunder, rumblings, lightning, and an earthquake take place. We noted in chapter six that these upheavals of nature signify that God is choosing to make His presence known.

Although we can't be absolutely certain of the meaning of these verses, it is clear that something monumental is happening differently for the saved and for those who have not chosen to be on God's side. Let us now delve into the seven trumpets and see what we can learn.

Revelation 8:6-13: The First Four Trumpets

> *6 Then the seven angels who had the seven trumpets prepared to sound them.*

For the next five verses we are going to read about weird and mysterious and violent destruction taking place. We need to ask ourselves whether the events sound like something a loving caring God chooses to make happen or are they more exposé of the kind of mayhem Satan and his angels are causing on the earth. Yes, God is involved. We saw that His angels are participating, but does that mean they cause the trouble, or at God's bidding do they restrain the wicked angels from doing more than God allows? Let's see what clues we can discover.

The First Trumpet sounded and there comes hail and fire mixed with blood hurled down to the earth. I have not found any other place in the Bible that talks about hail and fire and blood all mixed up together. Cold and hot and liquid do not seem like something that would be found at the same time. They are hurled down. That means they are forcefully thrown down. As a result of this strange mixture a third of the earth was burned up, a third of the trees were burned up and all the green grass was burned up. One third is mentioned two times. We find a lot of one thirds in the Seven Trumpets.

The Second Trumpet sounded and something like a huge burning mountain is thrown into the sea. As a result, a third of the sea turned to blood, a third of the sea creatures died, and a third of the ships were destroyed. A third shows up three more times. So far, that is five times that we have read one third.

The Third Trumpet sounded, and a great blazing star fell from the sky on a third of the rivers and on the streams of water, implying that it was also a third. The name of the star is Wormwood. A third of the waters turned bitter and many people died as a result. Wormwood is a poisonous plant. It can damage the nervous system and cause mental deterioration. So here we have two more thirds listed, plus an implied third. Now we are up to seven times that we have read one third.

The Fourth Trumpet sounded and there are many more thirds listed. A third of the sun, moon and stars, so a third of them turned dark. A third of the day and a third of the night were affected. That is six more times that a third is listed. Now we are up to 13 times that a third has been associated with one of the trumpets. Plus, that other implied third. There has been an avalanche of thirds in the trumpets.

Something is falling in each of the first three Trumpets:

    1st Trumpet: fire and hail and blood are hurled down on the earth

    2nd Trumpet: a huge mountain was thrown into the sea

    3rd Trumpet: a great blazing star fell from the sky

In the Fourth Trumpet it is the heavens that are affected. The sun, moon and stars all lose a third of their light. Consequently, day and night lose a third of their light.

Another way to express what has happened is to see where the damage took place:

    1st Trumpet – The earth is damaged

    2nd Trumpet – The sea is damaged

    3rd Trumpet – The water in rivers and streams is damaged

    4th Trumpet – The natural sources of light are damaged

Everything has been damaged!

It seems impossible to connect these events with history. In the Great Famine of 1315–1317, up to 25% of the people in Europe died. Bubonic Plague, called the Black Death, from 1346 to 1353 killed up to 60% of the people in North Africa, Europe and the Middle East. We don't find one third mentioned anywhere in history. So, if all this destruction is not literal historical events, we may need to think of all these thirds as code language for something. As we continue reading Revelation, I believe we will come across the key to understanding all these thirds.

Meanwhile, it seems the destruction is as bad as it can get. But verse 13 is a warning that worse is yet to come.

> *13 As I watched, I heard an eagle that was flying in midair call out in a loud voice: 'Woe! Woe! Woe to the inhabitants of the earth, because of the trumpet blasts about to be sounded by the other three angels!'*

Symbols in Chapter Eight

- **Trumpets:** In the Bible, trumpets were used for signaling the start of war or approaching enemies, or warning of danger. Trumpets were also used to signal the start of holy days and times of worship. More importantly, trumpets signal the approach of God. Whenever trumpets sounded, it reminded the Israelites that God is sovereign, and He is near them.

- **Prayers and Incense:** Jesus' righteousness added to our prayers assures us our prayers are heard in heaven and God is paying attention to them.

- **Hurling the censer on the earth:** This probably has something to do with God leaving people to reap the consequences of their own choices if they have not chosen to be on His side in the conflict. Nevertheless, His people are always assured of His presence and care.

- **Hail, fire, blood, a huge mountain and a blazing star** all fall down to earth causing enormous damage, but the damage was limited to one third. At this point we will keep thinking about whether God is causing the damage or whether He is limiting the damage being done. But as re-readers of Revelation, you may already be aware of what we will find in Revelation 12.

CHAPTER 9
THE FIFTH AND SIXTH TRUMPETS

In this day and age, we have all kinds of ways to send information to lots of people. There is television and radio and email and media mail and telephones with Amber Alerts and Tsunami warnings, and others I have not mentioned or maybe don't know about. In Bible times there were trumpets to call people's attention to something happening or being announced. In this verse we find an eagle screaming something across the sky. In Revelation 14 we will find angels crossing the sky calling out news in very loud voices.

Sometimes you will see a sign that says "Danger!" and then the sign adds what the danger is. That's what we have here. Eagles are the danger sign. They are big birds of prey. Their wingspan can be more than seven feet. (How tall is your father?) They have very sharp talons that allow them to pick up and carry whatever they have caught to eat. When I was very young, I read a book entitled "Elo the Eagle." One story in it was about an eagle carrying off a human baby. That was it for me. To this day I never sleep without a cover and never by a wide-open window, even though there is not an eagle alive that could carry me off! But I still associate eagles with danger.

Jesus Wins!   71

Here is something that everyone on earth needs to know. The eagle carries a dire message: "Woe, woe, woe." When the coming trumpets sound, we will read about even worse things than we have already encountered in the first four trumpets.

Revelation 9:1-12: The First Woe

> *1 The fifth angel sounded his trumpet, and I saw a star that had fallen from the sky to the earth. The star was given the key to the shaft of the Abyss.*

We hear the Fifth Trumpet sound its warning that something important is about to happen. Because this is the first woe, we know what happens will be very bad. The warning is about a star that fell from heaven, just like in the message of the Third Trumpet. But, remember repetition and enlargement, more information is about to be provided. It was given a key and allowed to take control of a place called the Abyss. The definition of the Abyss is a deep or seemingly bottomless chasm. Sometimes it is referred to as hell. Whatever it is, it is surely the opposite of God's beautiful creation. In Revelation 12 we will read a clear explanation of what or who this star is.

> *2 When he opened the Abyss, smoke rose from it like the smoke from a gigantic furnace. The sun and sky were darkened by the smoke from the Abyss.*

Now the star is being referred to as he, some kind of person or creature. The darkness reminds us of the darkness that took place under the Fourth Trumpet.

> *3 And out of the smoke locusts came down on the earth and were given power like that of scorpions of the earth.*

The smoke turns into locusts. There have been plenty of times when the sky has literally been darkened by millions of locusts that have descended on fields and eaten every plant, destroying the year's crop for the disappointed farmers. Those locusts have not been dangerous to humans, in fact, some people choose to eat them. But these symbolic locusts are different from the literal ones. These are like scorpions which can be very dangerous to humans. Their sting that carries the poison causes intense pain that lasts for hours, but usually does not kill you.

> *4 They were told not to harm the grass of the earth or any plant or tree, but only those people who did not have the seal of God on their foreheads.*

These dangerous locusts are very restricted in what they can do. They can't harm any kind of plant. They can only harm the people who do not have the seal of God that we read about in Revelation 7.

> *5 They were not allowed to kill them but only to torture them for five months. And the agony they suffered was like that of the sting of a scorpion when it strikes.*
>
> *6 During those days people will seek death but will not find it; they will long to die, but death will elude them.*

You have probably seen at least a picture of a scorpion with its long turned up tail that carries the stinger with its poison. If you actually see one, be very very careful to stay away from its tail. A sting causes intense pain. Here, where the sting is symbolic, the pain could last much longer and would ruin the life of the person who was stung. But this seems to be taking place after God's people have already been sealed indicating that they are soon going to heaven to live.

> *7 The locusts looked like horses prepared for battle. On their heads they wore something like crowns of gold, and their faces resembled human faces.*
>
> *8 Their hair was like women's hair, and their teeth were like lions' teeth.*
>
> *9 They had breastplates like breastplates of iron, and the sound of their wings was like the thundering of many horses and chariots rushing into battle.*
>
> *10 They had tails with stingers, like scorpions, and in their tails they had power to torment people for five months.*

Now John's vision is giving us further information about this smoke that turned into locusts, which were like scorpions. They are not small insects hopping along the ground. They look like war horses that have human faces, long hair, crowns, and very sharp teeth. They are wearing armor like soldiers would wear.

But they are still locusts because they have wings which make a thundering battle sound like you would only expect to hear during a war. They still have the scorpion tails that inject poison and torment people for a long time.

> *11 They had as king over them the angel of the Abyss, whose name in Hebrew is Abaddon and in Greek is Apollyon (that is, Destroyer).*

Now we are told that the star which fell and was given control of the Abyss is a king of the locusts and his name is revealed. It is given in both the Hebrew and the Greek languages so that everyone will be doubly sure who he is. The English translation of those two names is Destroyer. So, we have encountered war, an army, crowns, poison, teeth made to tear apart flesh. All of these are clues.

In the first four Trumpets we found out what damage and destruction was done. Now in this Fifth Trumpet, the first woe, we have received a lot more information about who causes the destruction. Do you suspect you might already know who these verses are talking about?

> *12 The first woe is past; two more woes are yet to come.*

Revelation 9:13-21: The Second Woe

> *13 The sixth angel sounded his trumpet, and I heard a voice coming from the four horns of the golden altar that is before God.*

Please go back and re-read Revelation 8:3, 4. As we begin to hear about the second woe, we are reminded of the many prayers of God's people that are being presented with incense by another angel. He was standing by the golden altar in front of God's throne showing that God is paying attention to the requests of His people.

The voice John heard could be this angel speaking, but the voice is coming from the four horns. In the Bible, horns symbolize power. Some scholars have thought that the voice might actually be Jesus Himself speaking. Whether the voice is that of the angel or Jesus, or symbolically the horns speaking, it is a powerful command being given in the next verse. It is coming from close by the throne of God and it will be obeyed.

> *14 It said to the sixth angel who had the trumpet, "Release the four angels who are bound at the great river Euphrates."*

This verse confirms that we are now reading about the Sixth Trumpet. When a trumpet sounds, it is an indication that something is going to happen. We need to pay attention and learn what it is.

First let's talk about the great river Euphrates. What do you know about this river? I hope you have maps in your Bible. Abraham would have followed the Euphrates River northwest from Ur when he left home following God's directions. He would have passed by the city of Babylon on his way.

In Daniel's time the Euphrates River flowed right through the middle of the city of Babylon. When it was near time for the Jewish people to return to Jerusalem at the end of the 70 years of captivity, the Medo-Persian general drained the river out into the desert so that his army could walk in shallow water into the middle of town through the gates that had been left open, and capture the city. The story of that night, from the viewpoint of what was happening in the palace, is found in Daniel 5. History books and archaeology tell us what was happening in and around the city that night.

A couple years later, King Cyrus set God's people free from Babylon. They were able to head home to Judea. Reading about the River Euphrates reminds us of Babylon and how God's people were rescued from there.

"Release the four angels" makes us question why angels would be bound or imprisoned. Were these good angels, or were they bad angels? And here is another third! In Revelation 7:2, 3, we read about God restraining evil. Now He is letting go of those restraints. I believe that tells us about these four angels. They are bad angels. There is a progression toward a climactic moment.

> *15 And the four angels who had been kept ready for this very hour and day and month and year were released to kill a third of mankind.*

So far, everything we have read about a third being damaged or destroyed has been limited or allowed by God but has been carried out by demonic forces. This is surely what is happening here. These angels have been bound in preparation for this very specific time when they will be allowed to kill one third of mankind. Now, during the Sixth Trumpet, they are released to accomplish their horrible job.

> *16 The number of the mounted troops was twice ten thousand times ten thousand. I heard their number.*

Here is a little math problem for you. Multiply ten thousand by ten thousand, and then double that number. What do you get? What???? Two hundred million! This is the number of soldiers on horses that appear in this army. That is huge! That is more than half of the people in the total United States of America. There is no army on earth that big. But John assures us he heard that number. If the four angels who are released are bad angels; they are associated with this army. So maybe this is the army of bad angels who want to fight against God's army. Maybe God's army is only that 144,000—not very good odds of winning. But don't worry. We already know that Jesus has won the war (Revelation 5:5,9,10. See 1 Samuel 14:6)

> *17 The horses and riders I saw in my vision looked like this: Their breastplates were fiery red, dark blue, and yellow as sulfur. The heads of the horses resembled the heads of lions, and out of their mouths came fire, smoke and sulfur.*

These riders are protected by colorful breastplates. The fiery red, dark blue and yellow are the same as what came out of the horses' mouths: fire, smoke and sulfur. Fire is red, sulfur is yellow. Have you ever heard that a room was blue with smoke?

> *18 A third of mankind was killed by the three plagues of fire, smoke and sulfur that came out of their mouths.*

It was what came out of the horses' mouths that killed people. Remember that only truth comes out of Jesus' mouth. This is death coming out of these horse's mouths.

> *19 The power of the horses was in their mouths and in their tails; for their tails were like snakes, having heads with which they inflict injury.*

You will never find one of these horses in your local zoo. These horses have two heads. The front head kills one third of the population. The back head is like a poisonous snake that could bite. This colossal army is totally protected! The riders are wearing armor. The horses are dangerous from the front and from the back. Surely, nobody can defeat this army! Don't be too sure. Just wait until we get to chapter nineteen and read about the opposing army.

> *20 The rest of mankind who were not killed by these plagues still did not repent of the work of their hands; they did not stop worshiping demons, and idols of gold, silver, bronze, stone and wood—idols that cannot see or hear or walk.*
>
> *21 Nor did they repent of their murders, their magic arts, their sexual immorality or their thefts.*

Nobody changed their mind. God's people have already been sealed, so they surely don't want to choose to be on the side of this destructive alliance. The two-thirds who survived but were in danger of being killed don't want to change their minds either. Maybe they are so afraid of the power of this king named Destroyer and his gigantic army that they are scared to even think about changing sides. And maybe they are determined to continue indulging in their favorite sins, no matter who gets hurt.

In verse 20 the sins are all related to their choice to not worship God. Instead, they chose to worship demons and the idols that represent them. Imagine the time and creativity and money that went into making and worshiping all those idols. They have deceived people into thinking that somehow or other they will be helped. Unnumbered people have prayed to them, begging for something they need or want. Sometimes supernatural things have happened. Maybe they have received numbers they can play on horse races, and they have won some money, but they haven't received answers to the sickness and worry and sadness that fills their lives.

Who is behind all these idols? Remember how desperately Satan wants to be worshiped. He has ways to make the powers of the idols seem real to the worshipers, but no real blessing takes place. The worshipers are left sick and worried and sad, and still under the power of Satan who only wishes to do them harm. They miss the joy of worshiping God who loves them and wants to bless them with a happy confident life.

Verse 21 relates that neither have they repented of the sins that hurt other people. Murder, sexual immorality, and stealing are the sixth, seventh and eighth commandments. When people chose to ignore how God wishes them to relate to other people, there are always victims. God knows every person who has been hurt, and He is always on the side of victims.

Here is a short explanation for why there is a law and why God asks us to follow it: "The law is an expression of the thought of God; when received in Christ, it becomes our thought. It lifts us above the power of natural desires and tendencies, above temptations that lead to sin. God desires us to be happy, and He gave us the precepts of the law that in obeying them we might have joy." *Desire of Ages*, page 308.

The law shows us what God is like. All the unrepentant people are missing out on the blessings and happiness that are provided to everyone who chooses to live God's way.

Between the sixth and seventh seals, there was a timeout to watch what the people on God's side were doing. Now we come to the same kind of timeout during the sixth trumpet. Long ago there was a funny song entitled, "Meanwhile, Back in the Jungle." The song went back and forth between the jungle and the States which presumably was a better or safer place. This is different, but somewhat the same. We are leaving the description of "the jungle" to read about God's people. Later we will focus again on those who are opposed to God and His people. In Revelation 7:1 we read that evil was being restrained in the Intermission between the 6th and 7th Seals. Now in Revelation 9:13-16 we read that there is a letting go of restraint on demonic forces.

Symbols in Chapter Nine

- **The word "woe":** describes great sorrow and distress. The warning eagle predicted that the messages of the last three Trumpets would be worse than those of the first four Trumpets. And the prediction comes true. The first four Trumpets describe how God's perfect creation of the earth and the heavens have been damaged by the rebellion that started in heaven. The woes are an exposé of the weird and demonic powers that cause death, danger and torment to the people who are under their control.

- **The smoke:** symbolizes the darkness that came in the sky and on the earth by the rebellion that started in heaven. Then the smoke materializes into insects.

- **Locusts/scorpions/horses:** symbolize Satan's army. At first it seems just to be a damaging nuisance. Then it becomes apparent it is poisonous and painful, then comes the total realization that it is huge and intends to win the war and kill off anyone who resists.

CHAPTER 10
THE SECOND INTERMISSION

Revelation 10:1-7: The Mystery of God Comes to Completion

> *1 Then I saw another mighty angel coming down from heaven. He was robed in a cloud, with a rainbow above his head; his face was like the sun, and his legs were like fiery pillars.*

Now we come again to an Intermission or a Timeout, just like we found between the 6th and 7th Seals. Revelation 10 and most of chapter 11 are a break between the 6th and the 7th Trumpets. Both the Intermission during the Seals and the Intermission during the Trumpets turn our attention to what is happening on God's side of the conflict. They show that God's people have an opportunity to get something right before the end comes with the 7th Seal and the 7th Trumpet. It is an opportunity for refocusing, for clarification as the people of God go forward in fulfilling their mission to the world.

CHAPTER 10   The Second Intermission

An awesome heavenly being who seems maybe to be divine now appears to John. You can find the same description in Daniel 10:5, 6. This is a VIP, a very important person, or maybe we should say a very important angel.

> *2 He was holding a little scroll, which lay open in his hand. He planted his right foot on the sea and his left foot on the land,*
>
> *3 and cried with a loud voice, as when a lion roars. When he cried out, seven thunders uttered their voices.*
>
> *4 Now when the seven thunders uttered their voices, I was about to write; but I heard a voice from heaven saying to me, "Seal up the things which the seven thunders uttered, and do not write them."*

John received messages from Seven Thunders and was about to write them down when a voice from heaven told him to seal them up and not write them down. The messages were given, and they were sealed up. That means that at some point they could be unsealed. For now, they remain a secret, but someday we will find out what these messages were.

> *5 The angel whom I saw standing on the sea and on the land raised up his hand to heaven*

Now we are again focused on the very important angel who is about to give another message.

> *6 and swore by Him who lives forever and ever, who created heaven and the things that are in it, the earth and the things that are in it, and the sea and the things that are in it, that there should be delay no longer,*
>
> *7 but in the days of the sounding of the seventh angel, when he is about to sound, the mystery of God would be finished, as He declared to His servants the prophets.*

This very important angel is giving a very important message. We will be blessed if we understand it. First, he swears by God the Creator, so we can know that the message is absolutely true. And what he swears is that there should be no more delay, but what he actually says in Greek is, "No more time." So, something important is coming to an end.

Time is very important in our lives. We pay attention to our birthdays and holidays, and some of us are noting days, and months, and hours, and even minutes and seconds. When we study prophecy, we learn a lot about time. But when we live in the new earth, there will be much less attention paid to time. When we are living forever, time will hardly matter. We will remember when it is time to get together to worship God or go to a special occasion. Beyond that, I'm not sure what meaning time will have in a perfect universe. There won't be any reason to count birthdays.

What is it that will happen when there is no more time? The mystery of God will be finished. What does that mean? It is a mystery about God, not about time. The angel says God already told His prophets about it, and now it will be brought to completion.

Let's go to Daniel 2. Four young Jewish men had just finished their Babylonian university education and had started working for the government. God chose that moment to reveal to a pagan king, Nebuchadnezzar, what would happen during the rest of world history. This is an amazing story that I hope you know very well. It is the ultimate mystery story because the king had forgotten the dream and demanded that someone tell him what he had dreamed, or he would kill all the wisemen. No human or demonic power was able to reveal it.

Daniel and his three friends prayed earnestly that God would reveal the mystery and save their lives. During the night in a vision, the dream and its meaning were revealed to Daniel. In the morning, he told the king what God had disclosed to him. The king was thrilled and recognized that the God of heaven was the God of gods, the Lord of kings and the revealer of mysteries.**

So, what was the mystery? It is mentioned eight times in Daniel 2, so in the king's mind it was big. Yes, there would be three world empires after his. No, there would be no more world empires after that, just a mixture of empires standing on feet of clay. Just to be able to tell what would happen thousands of years in the future is amazingly big and only possible for the sovereign God. But the biggest mystery was more than that. It is knowledge of the stone cut "without hands." (The word "human" is added by the translators.)

That is knowledge that no one else can have because they cannot think of it or even imagine it. It is knowledge that comes from the kind of person God is. The phrase can be translated, "Not by power," because hands represent a person's power. Daniel 2:34, 45. The mystery revealed to Nebuchadnezzar was the mystery of God. He will establish a kingdom without the use of power. It is the kingdom of the Lamb that was killed with violence.

Back in Revelation 10:6, 7, the mighty angel swears on God's name that there will be no more time. When the seventh angel is about to sound his trumpet, the mystery of God will be accomplished. Every part of Daniel 2 came true just as God predicted it would. The four world empires, followed by a mishmash of smaller nations that couldn't stick together or even get along with each other. Then how often do we think about the Kingdom of the Lamb Killed by Violence that will come true just as literally. It will not have any human intervention. It will be established without hands.

Prophetic time would be no more. The major lines of prophecy were finished. Now it would be the time of the end. There is no prophecy to tell us when Jesus will return the second time. His Second Coming will take place based on different circumstances, not based on prophetic time.

Remember that part of the book of Daniel had been sealed. (Daniel 12:4, 9) Very quickly, when the prophetic time of persecution ended, and the time of the end began, people all over the world began to study the book of Daniel. Already, by the 1820's, 2500 books and articles had been published. They were all endeavoring to explain the meaning of the prophecies in Daniel. This was the fulfillment of Daniel 12:4, "Many shall go here and there to increase knowledge."

Although it is true that lots of inventions around that time made it easier for people to travel, the verse is actually talking about people studying the book of Daniel, here and there, back and forth, so that knowledge about that book—which had been sealed for so long—was increased. Daniel 12:9 gives more information. The study of Daniel would be an enormous blessing to those who studied. "None of the wicked shall understand, but those who are wise will understand."

Revelation 10:8-11: The Angel and the Little Scroll

> *8 Then the voice that I had heard from heaven spoke to me once more: "Go, take the scroll that lies open in the hand of the angel who is standing on the sea and on the land."*

Again, John hears the voice that came from the horns of the altar of incense before the throne of God. (Revelation 9:13) Have you noticed how often we find that heaven is intimately involved in what is happening on earth? God and the angels are focused on us and what is best for us. That should give us a lot of comfort and assurance that all will be well.

> *9 So I went to the angel and asked him to give me the little scroll. He said to me, "Take it and eat it. It will turn your stomach sour, but 'in your mouth it will be as sweet as honey.'"*
>
> *10 I took the little scroll from the angel's hand and ate it. It tasted as sweet as honey in my mouth, but when I had eaten it, my stomach turned sour.*
>
> *11 Then I was told, "You must prophesy again about many peoples, nations, languages and kings."*

At this point in the book of Revelation, we need to pay attention to what is contained in the book of Daniel as well as in Revelation. Lots of bad news was given. God's people were persecuted by one kingdom after another. It was hard to see how Jesus would ever win.

Finally, here is good news to be devoured and internalized. Unfortunately, after savoring it for a little while, it ends up being a huge disappointment. It is like enjoying a delicious meal and then discovering that it makes you sick to your stomach.

You can find many books explaining what happened after the middle of the nineteenth century. There was huge expectation that Jesus was about to come. Stories from every continent except Antarctica tell of people learning from the Bible that Jesus' coming was near. But most of the stories come from the eastern United States. It was a time of great joy and deep Bible study. Somehow those who were studying did not see that the good news would be bitter after they had enjoyed eating it. Indeed, they were terribly disappointed when Jesus did not come as expected. Many thousands gave up their belief in Jesus' Second Coming and went back to life as usual.

A few were so certain that they had been blessed and guided in their Bible study, that they went back and studied the Bible even more. That was when they discovered the prediction of bitterness and the added instruction

CHAPTER 10   The Second Intermission

that they needed to again give the message to the world. It was hard to do, and they were very few in number at the beginning, but under God's guidance they began the task.

Symbols in Chapter Ten

- **The mighty angel:** looks like he could be Jesus, but probably he is an important angel

- **The little scroll:** open in his hand, is the book of Daniel which had been sealed but was now open for study

- **One foot on the sea and one foot on the land:** his message had world-wide importance.

- **No more time, or no more delay:** the prophetic time periods had ended

- **The mystery of God:** how by His power He can control the world's events without depriving anyone of freedom of choice, and can establish an eternal kingdom without force or human help

- **The scroll tasted like honey in John's mouth:** From the time of Daniel's prophecies, God's people had endured all kinds of persecution. It had been endless bad news. Now with the little scroll came the good news that Christ would soon come and restore His people to the harmony and perfection that God had intended for them.

- **Sour in his stomach:** There was bitter disappointment when Jesus did not come right away. Instead, His people had to follow His guidance in carrying the gospel again to the whole world before He could return to take His people to heaven.

CHAPTER 11
THE INTERMISSION AND THE SEVENTH TRUMPET

Revelation 11:1-2: Measuring the Temple

> *1 I was given a reed like a measuring rod and was told, "Go and measure the temple of God and the altar, with its worshipers.*
>
> *2 But exclude the outer court; do not measure it, because it has been given to the Gentiles (or nations). They will trample on the holy city for 42 months.*

We have now come to a particularly challenging chapter. It will be important to look very carefully at what we read. First, we read about places: The temple and the altar, then the outer court and the Holy City.

Here we find those who worship, and those who trample. Those who worship are inside the temple. Those who trample are outside.

Jesus Wins! **87**

Those who "trample," trample on those who worship. So, the spaces break down. The lines are blurred. Those who are outside can trample on the worshipers even though they are inside the temple. But God knows who are His, and He is always with His people.

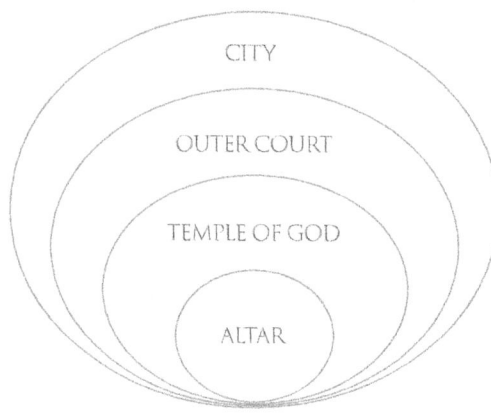

In the first six trumpets we found an exposé of demonic activity. Now in chapter 11, we are looking at what is happening from God's side of the conflict. No matter how terrible the events that are taking place, God is always working on behalf of His people. Looking at the big picture during those years, we can't always see that. But history tells us of many who remained faithful to God and did not give up their faith regardless of the persecution. If we could listen to them tell their personal stories, we would hear that God made Himself real to them during their difficult lives. He provided care and comfort and peace in the midst of chaos and tyranny.

Turning to examples in the Old Testament, in Ezekiel 40:3, is the beginning of a long measuring process that continues for several chapters. It has to do with the temple area. Ezekiel 42:20 says that the measuring is specifically to separate the holy from the common, just like the inside and the outside in Revelation 11:1-2.

In another example, in Zechariah 2:1-5, there is a man going to measure Jerusalem. But an angel is sent to tell him that Jerusalem cannot be measured because it will be bigger than anyone can imagine. It won't need walls because God Himself will be a wall of fire to protect it. The man who wanted to measure did not have a big enough conception of what God was planning. Also, God's wall of fire cannot be seen, and certainly cannot be measured by human understanding. Both Zechariah and Revelation are talking about evaluating not buildings but people. Here in Revelation, it is God's people who worship.

The outer court is not to be measured. It is occupied by those who are not God's people. They are trampling on those who worship. And yet, those who worship are in God's space. He is there with them, checking on them, keeping them in mind.

Just two verses at the beginning of Revelation 11 leave us with plenty of questions. But we will move on to the next two verses.

Revelation 11:3-14: The Two Witnesses

> *3 And I will appoint my two witnesses, and they will prophesy for 1,260 days, clothed in sackcloth."*
>
> *4 They are "the two olive trees" and the two lampstands, and "they stand before the Lord of the earth."*

Leaving the two kinds of spaces, we are introduced to two witnesses who will prophecy for 1260 days. If that were literal days, it would only be three and a half years. But remember, Revelation 1:1 stated that this would be a book of symbols. The word "signifies" in most Bible versions translates the word for symbols in the Greek language. It makes sense that the 1260 days are really referring to 1260 years.

The 1260 days/years are mentioned at least five times in Daniel and Revelation. Sometimes they are mentioned other ways, as forty-two months, or three and a half years. Sometimes as time, times and half a time. That has long been understood as one plus two plus a half, equaling three and a half. We won't completely understand why there was a need for this time period until we get to heaven. But it is clearly a long time with lots of persecution for God's people. We will study it more when we come to Revelation 12.

So, what could the two witnesses be? The best guess is the Old and New Testaments that make up the entire Bible. Throughout the long years of persecution, the Bible always witnessed to the truth about God. We are given several ways to think about this.

1. **They witnessed in sackcloth.** That was what people wore when they were mourning for those who died. This is evidence that lots of people were dying during this time. Dying from persecution. Dying from disease because this was not a time when healthful living was understood. It is also evidence that the message given by the two witnesses was mostly ignored.

2. **They are two olive trees.** During Bible times and for centuries afterward, in the Mediterranean area, olive trees provided olive oil for lamps. In the Bible, olive oil is often

a symbol for the Holy Spirit. In Zechariah 4:1-6 you can also read about a vision of lamps and two olive trees. The light they produce comes only from the Holy Spirit.

3. **They are two lampstands.** These held the lamps that depended on the olive oil to produce light. Lampstands (Revelation 1:20) and trees (9:4) are used to represent God's people.

4. **They stand before the Lord of the earth.** Satan wants to be lord of the earth, but he isn't, and he never has been, and he never will be. This earth is the property of the Lord in heaven.

Let's read on about these two witnesses in verses 5 and 6.

> *5 And if anyone wants to harm them, fire proceeds from their mouth and devours their enemies. And if anyone wants to harm them, he must be killed in this manner.*
>
> *6 These have power to shut heaven, so that no rain falls in the days of their prophecy; and they have power over waters to turn them to blood, and to strike the earth with all plagues, as often as they desire.*

These are very powerful witnesses! God does not allow them to be harmed. No matter how hard people tried to destroy the Bible or change what the Bible said, God always protected it.

When the Dead Sea Scrolls were discovered in the late 1940's, the scholars who studied them found to their surprise that the Bible had not changed in 2000 years. All through the years when the Bible was neglected or attacked, God protected it.

The prophet Elijah was the one who had power to shut up the heavens and keep the rain from falling for three and a half years. After that he called down fire from heaven. Then, just a short time later he was hiding in the cave and had an encounter with God. Yet God was not in the fire (1 Kings 19:11-12).

Moses was the one who turned water into blood and announced each of the ten plagues in Egypt. The Song of Moses, which is about triumphing over enemies, is also sung by the Lamb (Revelation 15:2-4).

Is Revelation 11 using hyperbole or a metaphor to talk about the Bible having fire coming out of its mouth to kill anyone who tries to harm it, during a time when many of God's people were being killed with fire? Remember that hyperbole is intentional exaggeration.

Is it using a metaphor of turning water into blood like Moses? We find that the evil forces in Revelation turn water into blood (8:9; 16:3), while Moses sings the same song as the Lamb. Remember that a metaphor is using something to explain something else by showing how they are similar, even though in reality they are not the same. Or we can say that a metaphor describes something in a way that isn't literally true but helps explain an idea or make a comparison.

What do we make of Elijah calling fire down from heaven, and then the evil side also making fire come down from heaven (Revelation 8:7-10; 13:13)?

The two witnesses, as well as Moses and Elijah, were all working under the direction and mandate of God. The reality is that the evil side imitates the work of God and tries to have the same power and tries to force people to do things their way. Even though the methods appear to be the same, they are not, and the outcome is vastly different.

Similar to the blurred spaces for worshipers and tramplers, with the two Witnesses we find a mingling of God's side and the evil one's side. So far in Revelation 11, we have seen a mingling or blurring of the holy and the common. Measuring does not find a clear difference between, or separation of, the two. We will move on to verses 7 and 8.

> *7 Now when they have finished their testimony, the beast that comes up from the Abyss will attack them, and overpower and kill them.*
>
> *8 Their bodies will lie in the public square of the great city—which is figuratively called Sodom and Egypt—where also their Lord was crucified.*

In Revelation 11:3, we read that the Witnesses would prophecy for 1260 days. Here they have finished their testimony, so the 1260 days must have ended, or were just about to end, though they still have a bit more witnessing to do. Even though they had so much power during the time they were prophesying, now they are killed. It is interesting that in Greek the wording is, "their dead body" (singular) that shows how they are essentially one Bible, not the separate Old and New Testaments.

Do we know who the beast is who killed them? He is a familiar figure from the fifth Trumpet. Revelation 9:1 says a star fell from the sky and was given the key to the Abyss. Revelation 9:11 says the angel of the Abyss is king over the evil forces and his name is Destroyer. So, we know several things about him:

1. He fell from the sky; in other words, he fell from heaven.
2. He is in charge of the Abyss where all the evil armies come from.
3. He is an angel.
4. He is king of the evil forces.
5. His name is Destroyer.

If you still have any question about who he actually is, just wait until we come to Revelation 12.

Now moving on to the next verse, to not be buried is the height of humiliation in much of the world, even today. The dead are often buried the same day they die. The dead bodies of the two witnesses lay in the middle of the city for three and a half days. Added to the tragedy of their death is the disgrace of no burial.

Verse 8 tells us where this happened. It was in a great city. Symbolically it was called Sodom and Egypt. These two places rejected God entirely. Not even ten righteous people could be found in Sodom (Genesis 18:32). In Egypt, although he wavered, the Pharoah rejected any message from God through the deepening destruction of ten plagues (Exodus 7 to 11). So, notice that this is not literally talking about Sodom or Egypt.

Verse 8 goes on to say, "where also their Lord was crucified." That, of course, would be just outside Jerusalem which was supposed to be a Holy City. So, here again we find a mingling of the holy and the common—or in this case the violent evil. The witnesses suffered the same fate as did Jesus. Equally, these verses are not literally referring to Jerusalem.

> *9 For three and a half days some from every people, tribe, language and nation will gaze on their bodies and refuse them burial.*

> **10** *The inhabitants of the earth will gloat over them and will celebrate by sending each other gifts, because these two prophets had tormented those who live on the earth.*

During the three and a half days that the witnesses are dead, some people from all over the earth will gaze at them and agree they should not be buried. The word some means that not everyone agreed with the humiliation and disrespect. Some approved of what was happening.

More than just gazing and the lack of respect, they triumphed in the fact that the Two Witnesses were dead. They celebrated and sent gifts to each other. They were glad that these nuisances were dead and would not irritate them anymore. The witnesses had tormented them by making them feel guilty, by constantly bothering their consciences. What a surprise they had coming!

> **11** *But after the three and a half days the breath of life from God entered them, and they stood on their feet, and terror struck those who saw them.*
>
> **12** *Then they heard a loud voice from heaven saying to them, "Come up here." And they went up to heaven in a cloud, while their enemies looked on.*

After the three and a half days of merriment at the expense of the Two Witnesses, to the horror of the crowds, God resurrected them. Instantly the laughter and joy disappeared as great fear fell upon the crowds.

Their shocking experience continued. Now they heard the voice of God saying, "Come up here." God's voice is like rolling thunder, so strong and loud that everyone, even the deaf, are stopped in their tracks to hear it. At the sound of His voice, the Two Witnesses rose off the earth in a cloud, just like Jesus did at His ascension into heaven. All those who had cheered at their death saw this happen. Their guilty consciences returned with a vengeance, only multiplying their fear. More was yet to come.

> **13** *At that very hour there was a severe earthquake and a tenth of the city collapsed. Seven thousand people were killed in the earthquake, and the survivors were terrified and gave glory to the God of heaven.*

> **14 The second woe has passed; the third woe is coming soon.**

As the crowds stood contemplating what they had seen and heard, without warning they were engulfed in a tremendous earthquake that sent buildings reeling and falling all around them, killing many of them. After just a few minutes it became obvious to the survivors what had happened. They had escaped with their lives, but nothing would ever be the same again.

Mankind could not have caused this to happen. God was sovereign and He had spoken and put a stop to the wickedness around them. Like the pagan King Nebuchadnezzar, when Daniel had revealed and explained his dream, all those still alive now realize what they had ignored before. God was omnipotent and totally in charge. They willingly praised Him for being above all other powers, for acting with wisdom, and for saving their lives, giving them another opportunity to turn wholeheartedly to Him.

In the symbols for chapter eleven below, you will find a clear explanation of where the events with the two witnesses took place.

This is the end of the Sixth Trumpet, the second woe. The third woe, the Seventh Trumpet will follow shortly.

Revelation 11:15-19: The Seventh Trumpet

> **15 The seventh angel sounded his trumpet, and there were loud voices in heaven, which said:**
>
> **"The kingdom of the world has become the kingdom of our Lord and of his Messiah, and he will reign for ever and ever."**
>
> **16 And the twenty-four elders, who were seated on their thrones before God, fell on their faces and worshiped God,**

We are going to see that the Seventh Trumpet is all about rejoicing and worship that is happening in heaven. However, it is also the third woe. We will see below that this means it will be exceedingly bad news in two ways for the wicked who will not share in the joy of God's triumph over evil. It will finally sink into their brains that they bet on the wrong horse and have lost everything, while the friends of God are forever saved from persecution and death, to live forever in the harmony of God's kingdom.

The loud voices in heaven are rejoicing that the controversy is over, sin has been stopped in its tracks. Jesus has won. His victory is now being celebrated. The twenty-four elders who sit on thrones around God's throne, are so overcome with joy and praise that they fall face-down to worship God. In verses 17 and 18 we read what they say.

> *17 saying:*
> *"We give thanks to you, Lord God Almighty,*
>   *the One who is and who was,*
> *because You have taken your great power*
>   *and have begun to reign.*
>
> *18 The nations were angry,*
>   *and Your wrath has come.*
> *The time has come for judging the dead,*
>   *and for rewarding Your servants the prophets*
> *and Your people who revere Your name,*
>   *both great and small—*
> *and for destroying those who destroy the earth."*

The twenty-four elders are overwhelmed with praise for the kind of God they serve, who has now taken full control of the situation and shown His power and might. In Revelation chapters 4 and 5, they were perplexed because God wasn't using His power to overcome the wicked. Now they can see that His plan was to use truthful words and freedom of choice to draw people to freely choose which side they would believe and trust.

Now their choices have been made, and God ends the opportunity for anyone to switch sides. Remember that God's wrath is not like human wrath. It is not a time for Him to yell and fight and stamp His feet. God's wrath is the time when He turns sadly away from people He would have loved to save, but they did not choose to be on His side. When He turns away, they are left to the entire power of the evil side. So the third woe is horrible in two different ways. First, the wicked realize what they lost in not choosing God's side. Second, they will now be entirely at the mercy of evil angels who will no longer have any restraints put upon them.

The twenty-four elders continue their praise by saying there are still three things to be done. It is time to judge the dead, to reward those on God's side, and to destroy those who destroy the earth. These events will take place after the second coming of Jesus when we are with Him in heaven. But before that can happen, there must be decisions made about who will be rewarded. That has to happen while God's people are still here on earth.

After the heavenly time of judgment has passed, then it will be time for the executive judgment that culminates in the final destruction of the wicked. We will talk more about that later in the book.

The final verse of Revelation 11 provides a scene that is visible both in heaven and on earth.

> *19 Then God's temple in heaven was opened, and within his temple was seen the ark of his covenant. And there came flashes of lightning, rumblings, peals of thunder, an earthquake and a severe hailstorm.*

The ark of the covenant was first constructed at Sinai for the tent tabernacle (Exodus 37:1-9). After hundreds of years, it was moved into Solomon's temple (1 Kings 8:1-21). After a few more hundred years it was hidden just before the Babylonian captivity. It has never been seen since. That hiding place has never been found. Here is a paragraph that describes what happened to it.

> "Among the righteous still in Jerusalem, to whom had been made plain the divine purpose, were some who determined to place beyond the reach of ruthless hands the sacred ark containing the tables of stone on which had been traced the precepts of the Decalogue. This they did. With mourning and sadness, they secreted the ark in a cave, where it was to be hidden from the people of Israel and Judah because of their sins, and was to be no more restored to them. That sacred ark is yet hidden. It has never been disturbed since it was secreted." Prophets and Kings, 453:2

Now it shows up in the heavenly temple. It can even be seen—whether literally or intellectually—from earth.

In Old Testament times, the daily activities of the sanctuary were in the Holy Place. Only one day a year the activity centered in the Most Holy Place. So, most of the activities were in the Holy Place. Only a short period of time was spent in the Most Holy Place.

After the 1260 days/years when God's work of intercession in heaven was forgotten or ignored, the time came when people began to understand the importance of the activities in heaven. A few people came to understand and teach others the change that took place in heaven when the long period of 2300 days/years ended in 1844. This event helps us place the time in history when the Seventh Trumpet began to sound.

Remember that when all these events of nature happen together, it is a signal that God is about to reveal Himself. Something tremendous is about to happen.

Symbols in Chapter Eleven

- **"Measure" and "temple":** These are metaphors for people and what they are doing. There is judgment being made about people's relationship to God. This is an expansion on the "prophecying again" in chapter 10. Because it is sanctuary language, it also means that studying the sanctuary would be part of the final message to the world.

- **1260 days, and 42 months, and 3 ½ years, and time, times and half a time:** All these are ways that Daniel and Revelation refer to the period of persecution of God's people. The Bible frequently uses day and year as equivalent, so Bible scholars have long considered that each of these terms can refer to the 1260 years of persecution.

- **Dead body in the street for 3 ½ days:** The French Revolution, primarily in the city of Paris, and in the country of France, outlawing religion as they knew it, on November 26, 1793, abolished the Christian religion and set aside the Bible.[20] First they outlawed all religions, including Christianity, except for the worship of Reason. They substituted a ten-day week for the seven-day week. This was an initial period of pure atheism.

On May 9, 1794, the leadership, under the influence of Robespierre, modified the pure atheism to the worship of the Supreme Being. The problem was that the Supreme Being to which they referred was nature,

---
[20] *Andrews University Seminary Studies, Vol. 47, No. 1, 117-134*

CHAPTER 11   The Intermission And The Seventh Trumpet

and a dancing girl from the opera was presented as the goddess of Reason. It turned out that Robespierre himself wanted to be worshiped and did receive similar honor as the goddess. That disgusted many prominent politicians, and Robespierre himself died by the guillotine a few weeks later.

On July 18, 1797, the laws against Christianity and the Bible were rescinded. Immediately there was an unexpected resurgence in Christian faith and practice. This was a clear example of the prophetic 3 ½ days/3 ½ years that the Bible lay dead in the streets. When that time ended, Bible societies were established, and millions of Bibles were printed in many languages. The unsealed book of Daniel was earnestly studied, and the second coming of Jesus was discovered and began to be preached.

PART IV
THE COSMIC CONFLICT
FROM A TO Z

At last, we have come to the middle of Revelation. Half of the book is before, and half comes after. It will be helpful to think of this as the top of a pyramid. In Revelation 12, we will find a summary of the big picture of what started all the trouble on earth, what God did about it, and how it will conclude. It will help us to understand what we have already read, and it will also cast light on what we will be reading later. To understand the Cosmic Conflict, we need to see Revelation 12-14 as the context for what happens from Revelation 4 right down to Revelation 20 and beyond. Chapter 13 reveals what Satan does to try to win the war. Then Chapter 14 will show us how God does win the war.

At the beginning of Revelation 4, John looked through the open door into heaven. We are right there with him, looking over his shoulder as he writes what he sees. Throughout Revelation, down to chapter 20, John continues to watch something like a wide-screen movie that reveals the actions of Satan and shows the actions of God in the context of the proceedings in the heavenly council. We get to see that movie as well, as we continue to study this monumental concluding book of the Bible.

Remember that we need to bear in mind a couple of ideas about the way John sees and writes the story. The first is repetition and enlargement. The Seven Trumpets repeated the same timeframe as the Seven Seals, but it enlarged on different aspects of the story. We will see that again. The Bible frequently uses that literary device. Genesis 2 enlarges on Genesis 1, but with a different emphasis. Daniel 2 and 7 and 8 and 11 cover the same time periods but enlarge on different parts of the story.

Jesus Wins! 99

PART 4   The Cosmic Conflict From A To Z

Another idea that can confuse us if we don't understand, is why John doesn't write things in chronological order. In Bible times, people liked to know first what was going to happen at the end of the story. Then they could concentrate on the events that led to the end. That is called reasoning from effect to cause. Most of us like to wait for the ending to be a surprise. That is called reasoning from cause to effect. That is the reason that in several chapters in Revelation, we are told about what will happen in heaven in the future. Then we read more about what leads up to that future event.

CHAPTER 12

PART 1: THE WOMAN AND THE DRAGON

This chapter summarizes the entire story of the cosmic conflict. Further details are given in other chapters. Here is a brief chart to simplify what we are going to read.

Verses	Subject
Revelation 12:1-2	The woman
Revelation 12:3-4	The dragon
Revelation 12:5	The short story of Jesus
Revelation 12:6	The woman
Revelation 12:7-9	Short story of the dragon
Revelation 12:10-11	Celebration in heaven
Revelation 12:12-13	The dragon
Revelation 12:14-16	The woman
Revelation 12:17; 13:1	The dragon

Revelation 12:1-4: Two Great Signs

The first part of Revelation 12 begins with two great signs, but they are not in chronological order. Remember that as we read verses 1 and 2.

> *1 A great sign appeared in heaven: a woman clothed with the sun, with the moon under her feet and a crown of twelve stars on her head.*
>
> *2 She was pregnant and cried out in pain as she was about to give birth.*

In the Bible a woman represents the church, God's people. Because it will be obvious that the baby to be born is Jesus, we will think of His mother Mary as the woman. But the meaning here is much broader. The people on God's side are shown here as in pain, but greatly honored by God, being clothed with the sun and the stars, while standing on the moon.

> *3 Then another sign appeared in heaven: an enormous red dragon with seven heads and ten horns and seven crowns on its heads.*
>
> *4 Its tail swept a third of the stars out of the sky and flung them to the earth. The dragon stood in front of the woman who was about to give birth, so that it might devour her child the moment he was born.*

This second sign actually started much earlier, because it is referring to Satan who rebelled against God while he was still the most exalted angel in heaven. He was not satisfied to be a created being. He wanted to be God. By his slander and insinuation against God, he eventually persuaded one third of the angels to side with him. A third of the angels! Does that wave any red flags in your mind? Maybe this is the explanation for all the thirds we read about during the trumpets. Maybe those were hints to help us realize who was responsible for the destruction of people and nature.

Revelation 12:5-6: The Baby and the Woman

When Satan realized that God was to be born on earth, he did everything in his power to kill baby Jesus, or later, to tempt Him to sin. First, he used King Herod who killed all the baby boys in Bethlehem. But God had warned Joseph to go to Egypt, so baby Jesus was saved. Let's continue to read to see what happened.

> *5 She gave birth to a son, a male child, who "will rule all the nations with an iron scepter." And her child was snatched up to God and to his throne.*

So, Jesus was born, and He was protected from the dragon and went back to heaven to join God on His throne. That is the very short version of the story.

Notice that the center part of the verse is in quotes. It is a reference from Psalm 2:9. Let's read both verses 8 and 9 in **Psalm 2**.

> *8 Ask me,*
> *and I will make the nations your inheritance,*
> *the ends of the earth your possession.*
> *9 You will break them with a rod of iron;*
> *you will dash them to pieces like pottery."*

This is a prophecy about Jesus. He was the Creator, so He will ultimately have dominion over everything on earth. The next line could be translated, "You will rule/shepherd them with a rod of iron." A shepherd carried an iron rod to protect the sheep from wild animals that wanted to kill them.

When pottery falls and breaks to pieces, it cannot be repaired. It is totally destroyed. This is referring to the tragic ending of those who don't choose to be on God's side at the end of time.

Now back to **Revelation 12**:

> *6 The woman fled into the wilderness to a place prepared for her by God, where she might be taken care of for 1,260 days.*

Jesus went back to heaven, but the woman, the Church, needed to be cared for during the difficult 1260 days/years of persecution that lay ahead. God prepared a place for her in the wilderness, an area where few people lived, where she would be safer. 1 Kings 17:3-6 tells the story of Elijah who was cared for when his life was in danger. God directed him to an isolated place where he had a brook for water and ravens fed him twice a day.

Revelation 12:7-9: How the War Started

Now we come to the three verses in the middle of Revelation 12 that start the second part of the chapter. Chronologically this would have come first. They show us what happened thousands of years ago in heaven that resulted in Lucifer losing his innocence and sin entering this earth.

> *7 Then war broke out in heaven. Michael and his angels fought against the dragon, and the dragon and his angels fought back.*
>
> *8 But he was not strong enough, and they lost their place in heaven.*
>
> *9 The great dragon was hurled down—that ancient serpent called the devil, or Satan, who leads the whole world astray. He was hurled to the earth, and his angels with him.*

Michael seems to be the name given to Jesus when He is the commander in chief of the armies of heaven. We find the name a few places in the Bible. Michael accepts worship, so we know for sure that He is a divine being.

Lucifer wanted to be God. He was jealous of Jesus who was God. He thought of his own extraordinary beauty and influence and was confident he would be a better God. He whispered to anyone who would listen to him that God was unfair, arbitrary, unforgiving and severe. One third of the angels fell for his lies. Finally, they tried to take over heaven. Then Jesus and those on his side had to ensure the future of the universe. Isaiah 14:12-15 is the background text that shows Lucifer to be the light bearer, a brilliant star, brilliant enough to be seen in daylight, the leader of the angels in heaven, who rebelled against his high position and wanted to be like God. (Lucifer is another translation for "shining one, son of dawn.") He was cast out and will finally be destroyed. That is the whole story of Lucifer/Satan in brief.

Revelation 12:7 says, "war broke out." The Greek word translated "war" is the word usually translated "polemics". Polemics is the art or practice of engaging in controversial debate or dispute. This was a war of words, not a battle with hand-to-hand fighting. It was a disagreement about how heaven should be governed. It was a disagreement about what kind of person God is. This was not a military conflict.

Verse nine has four words that characterize what Satan and his followers were doing.

1. **The great dragon:** We have already read that it had seven heads, and ten horns, and seven crowns on the heads. We will find this same description again later.
2. **"Ancient serpent":** takes our thoughts right back to the Garden of Eden where he deceived Eve and wrested control of this earth. (Genesis 3:1,13, 15) There in verse 1, Satan misrepresented God as a harsh unreasonable person. In verse 13, Eve says he deceived her. Verse 15 reveals who will win in the conflict between Christ and Satan
3. **Devil:** in Greek is *diabolos* and can be translated slanderer or mudslinger.
4. **Satan:** in Greek is *ho satanas* which can be translated adversary.

And then for good measure, to be sure we understand as much as possible, verse 9 goes on to say that he leads the whole world astray. He is the deceiver: It is clear that the rebellion in heaven was about words and attitudes and disagreements that could not continue to exist together.

The evil angel could not be allowed to continue bullying all the intelligent beings throughout the universe. They had decided to stay on God's side even though they might still have some questions. Lucifer, who became the dragon/the serpent/ Satan/the devil/the deceiver and his followers were using lies and innuendo, trying to destroy God's reputation, because they did not have a good case that could be shown to be true.

Yet God proved that He was not the way they said He was, by being fair even to his enemies. They were forced out of heaven but allowed to come to this earth. Satan still had some influence throughout the universe until Jesus died on the cross.[21] That event showed all the intelligent beings throughout the cosmos how evil he really was. After that, they would never again be influenced by his lies.

If Adam and Eve had kept their trust in God, then Satan and his minions would not long have had access to them to tempt them. Since our first parents so rapidly fell for Satan's lies, he and his cohorts felt sure they could ultimately win the war and control all of this earth, even if they had lost the universe.

---

[21] *John 12:31*

Revelation 12:10-12: A Joyful Celebration In Heaven, But Woe To the Earth

Beginning in verse 10 we will see what was happening after Jesus returned to heaven and Satan had lost his influence throughout the cosmos. There was celebration because Jesus had triumphed. However, Satan is now even more dangerous for the earth because he is furious knowing that he has limited time to gain control.

> *10 Then I heard a loud voice in heaven say:*
>
> *"Now have come the salvation and the power*
> *and the kingdom of our God,*
> *and the authority of his Messiah.*
> *For the accuser of our brothers and sisters,*
> *who accuses them before our God day and night,*
> *has been hurled down.*
>
> *11 They triumphed over him*
> *by the blood of the Lamb*
> *and by the word of their testimony;*
> *they did not love their lives so much*
> *as to shrink from death.*
>
> *12 Therefore rejoice, you heavens*
> *and you who dwell in them!*
> *But woe to the earth and the sea,*
> *because the devil has gone down to you!*
> *He is filled with fury,*
> *because he knows that his time is short."*

Revelation 12:13-17: Satan's Continuing War Against the Woman

This brings us to the third part of chapter 12, the final section, verses 13–17. Here we find the summary of Satan's continuing war. This is the beginning of the end as Satan, having lost his influence throughout the rest of the universe, tries desperately to destroy God's people here on earth.

> *13 When the dragon saw that he had been hurled to the earth, he pursued the woman who had given birth to the male child.*

> *14 The woman was given the two wings of a great eagle, so that she might fly to the place prepared for her in the wilderness, where she would be taken care of for a time, times and half a time, out of the serpent's reach.*
>
> *15 Then from his mouth the serpent spewed water like a river, to overtake the woman and sweep her away with the torrent.*
>
> *16 But the earth helped the woman by opening its mouth and swallowing the river that the dragon had spewed out of his mouth.*

These final verses of chapter 12, except for the very last verse, describe how Satan has tried to kill God's people ever since Jesus went back to heaven. Remember that time, times, and half a time are another way of referring to 1 plus 2 plus a half. When you add those together you have 3 ½. If those refer to days, that is not much time. In prophecy, in the books of Daniel and Revelation, a year is 360 days. Each day is a real year. So, 360, plus 2 x 360, plus half of 360 is 1260 days/years (360 + 720 + 180 = 1260 years).

Since Satan wasn't able to kill Jesus, he went after the Woman, God's faithful people. They were guided quickly—like flying on eagles' wings—into places that were safer from Satan and his followers.

The mention of eagles' wings can take us back to Exodus 19:4 where God tells Moses what to say to the Israelites.

> *4 You yourselves have seen what I did to Egypt, and how I carried you on eagles' wings and brought you to myself.*

Here God is referring to the miracles He performed to rescue His people from Egypt and to lovingly care of them on their way to Canaan. Isaiah also refers to eagles' wings in **Isaiah 40:31**.

> *But those who hope in the LORD will renew their strength. They will soar on wings like eagles; they will run and not grow weary, they will walk and not be faint.*

If you have ever seen an eagle soaring through the sky with its powerful broad wings, you can imagine how this was a good illustration for God to use in describing He guidance and care for His people.

"... water like a river, to overtake the woman and sweep her away with the torrent," refers to the armies of enemies that were sent to force God's people to conform or be destroyed. They suffered fierce persecution for their faithfulness to Jesus, but the earth helped them by making it very difficult and dangerous for the armies to find and kill them. The earth served as a protecting force, guarding a safe space for the Woman.

Psalm 124:2-5 shows how the same illustration was used in the Old Testament to portray God's care.

> *2. If the LORD had not been on our side*
> *when people attacked us,*
>
> *3. they would have swallowed us alive*
> *when their anger flared against us;*
>
> *4. the flood would have engulfed us,*
> *the torrent would have swept over us,*
>
> *5. the raging waters*
> *would have swept us away.*

Genesis 4:10-12 is another Old Testament passage that shows that the earth is a participant in what God is doing. The earth is on God's side and is a kind of caring figure or protecting force for His people.

> *10. The LORD said, "What have you done? Listen! Your brother's blood cries out to me from the ground.*
>
> *11. Now you are under a curse and driven from the ground, which opened its mouth to receive your brother's blood from your hand.*
>
> *12. When you work the ground, it will no longer yield its crops for you. You will be a restless wanderer on the earth."*

Numbers 16 also tells a tragic story of rebellion, and the earth opening its mouth to swallow the leaders of the rebellion. In that story also the earth was a participant in God's judgment.

Coming to the last verse of chapter 12, we are "the rest of her offspring" and should not be surprised when we are harassed by Satan. But what does he plan to do now?

> *17 Then the dragon was enraged at the woman and went off to wage war against the rest of her offspring—those who keep God's commands and hold fast their testimony about Jesus. (emphasis supplied)*

Satan's target is still the same—God's people. But he is going to do something different, he is going to change his tactics. The phrase, "went off" in the verse really means he went away and didn't tell where he was going. In other words, he disappeared to attack God's people, the Woman, with a different approach. In chapter 12 we have first seen that he tried direct confrontation, working to destroy Jesus and then the Woman, but that didn't work. We will learn about his new strategy in Revelation 13.

Before we leave chapter 12, we will look at the phrase, "those who keep God's commands and hold fast their testimony about Jesus." Almost this exact same phrase appears six times in Revelation.

1. **Revelation 1:2** – the word of God and the testimony of Jesus Christ
2. **Revelation 1:9** – the word of God and the testimony of Jesus Christ
3. **Revelation 6:9** – the word of God and the testimony they had maintained
4. **Revelation 12:17** – who keep God's commands and hold fast their testimony about Jesus
5. **Revelation 14:12** – who keep His commands and remain faithful to Jesus
6. **Revelation 20:4** – because of their testimony about Jesus and because of the word of God

It is obvious that there is a very close connection between the two; and God's people are connected to both. Satan's misrepresentation of God is defeated by Jesus' revelation of God and His commandments. When Jesus came to this earth to show what God is like, He defeated Satan. It was by His death—the Lamb that was killed with violence—that He won the war. When we faithfully testify to the goodness of God like Jesus did, we are His partners in winning the war.

Satan is desperately trying to sever the connection between God's word and Jesus' testimony. And He does this by trying to separate us from God's word and the testimony of Jesus. Each of these places is talking about God's word in relation to how it has been revealed by Jesus' testimony or Jesus' faithfulness.

Symbols in Chapter Twelve

- **The woman:** The symbol for God's people, is highly honored by being clothed with the sun, standing on the moon and with a crown of twelve stars. Remember that earlier in the book stars were symbols for the leaders of God's people.

- **An enormous red dragon:** Satan is described in multiple ways and more clearly identified than any other symbol in the Bible.

- **One third of the stars:** These are the angels who fell for Satan's slander and lies and were exiled to this earth with him.

- **The woman's child:** Jesus who came to this earth as the promised Messiah. Satan tried to kill him, but He completed His mission and returned to heaven.

- **The war in heaven:** A war of words, not an armed conflict. This was a war of charging God with being unfair. Satan was jealous of Jesus and wanted to be God himself, rather than accepting his place as a created being. The animosity became so intense that both sides could not remain in the same place. Satan and his followers were forced out of heaven.

- **Water like a river:** Symbolized the armies that were sent to force God's people to comply with laws that forbade them to remain faithful to Jesus. If they couldn't be forced to comply, they would be killed.

- **The earth helped them:** God directed His people to remote places to live where they would be safe. These remote places were unsafe for the armies who would pursue them.

- **The rest of her offspring:** God's people remain the ones who Satan is furious at and trying to deceive and kill. That is referring to us. Remember that God is far more powerful and will be with us as we maintain our faith and trust in Him.

CHAPTER 13
THE BIG PICTURE OF THE COSMIC CONFLICT, PART 2

This is an enlargement and continuation of the big picture of the Cosmic Conflict. Revelation 13 reveals Satan's new strategy to separate people from God during the end-time. As we have seen in Revelation so far, this book is often an exposé of Satan's activity to help us understand what has happened and what is happening around us.

Revelation 13:1-10: The Beast from the Sea

> *1 The dragon stood on the shore of the sea. And I saw a beast coming out of the sea. It had ten horns and seven heads, with ten crowns on its horns, and on each head a blasphemous name.*

In the last verse of chapter 12 we read that the dragon went away to change his tactics. Here in the first verse of chapter 13 he is standing on the shore of the sea. But look what comes out of the water. A beast that looks just like the dragon! Comparing Revelation 12:3, we see the same heads and horns and crowns.

Jesus Wins! 111

We need to think about the blasphemous names. Blasphemous means "against God or sacred things". These names on the heads are saying something bad about God. It is a clue that this beast has something to do with false religion.

> *2 The beast I saw resembled a leopard but had feet like those of a bear and a mouth like that of a lion. The dragon gave the beast his power and his throne and great authority.*

Leopards, bears, and lions were unclean animals in Jewish thinking. Even though the blasphemous names indicated something about religion, the animal parts reveal this was an unclean or impure beast.

To understand what is happening in this verse, we have to go back to the Old Testament, to Daniel 7. The prophet Daniel had a vision at night of four beasts that came up out of the Mediterranean Sea. The first was like a lion, the second was like a bear, the third was like a leopard, and the fourth was a terrifying, frightening, powerful beast that had ten horns. Now in Revelation 13 we see a beast come out of the sea that has characteristics of all four of the beasts that Daniel saw. Then the verse tells us that the dragon gave the beast his power and his throne and great authority. This is Satan's Plan B. Instead of revealing himself, he hides behind the beast.

> *3 One of the heads of the beast seemed to have had a fatal wound, but the fatal wound had been healed. The whole world was filled with wonder and followed the beast.*

We find over and over again in Revelation that Satan was imitating Jesus in order to get people to worship him. John 12:20-33 relates an interesting event that took place just a few hours before the Passover supper with the disciples. Some Greeks (Gentiles) had come to Jerusalem for the Passover, and they wanted to see Jesus. During His meeting with them, in verses 31-33 Jesus explains what was about to happen. "'Now is the time for judgment on this world; now the prince of this world will be driven out. And I, when I am lifted up from the earth, will draw all people to myself.' He said this to show the kind of death he was going to die."

When Adam sinned, he lost his place as prince of this world. Satan stole that from him. But Jesus revealed that His death would drive out Satan.

We can be sure that Satan paid close attention to Jesus' words. After the crucifixion and resurrection, Satan watched how Jesus' words were coming true. Many many people were drawn to believe in the Lamb that was killed with violence, and to faithfully follow Him. Therefore, if Satan wanted to retain any power and influence, his side in the conflict also needed a fatal wound that was healed. He had now totally lost his power and influence throughout the universe, but there was still hope that he could control this world.

He had lost his place in heaven, then he had lost his influence in the universe. Jesus' death on the cross had given Satan a death blow. To maintain his power by imitating Jesus, he needed to figure out how to turn this death blow to his advantage so that it increased his influence over people on this earth. He would do that by working through the beast to force people to submit to his will.

Fast forward almost two thousand years and you find that there was a plan by the government of France to destroy the beast. The plan was carried out and everyone thought it was successful, but it was not. Two years later the beast was resuscitated a little bit. Then, after years of appearing to be near death, gradually over time, the beast regained its life and power. Its wound will not be completely healed until it is powerful enough to again persecute and kill God's people. We are living during the time that Satan and the beast wait for the complete healing of the wound.

> *4 People worshiped the dragon because he had given authority to the beast, and they also worshiped the beast and asked, "Who is like the beast? Who can wage war against it?"*

Satan succeeded in his intentions, because when people were worshiping the beast, they were really worshiping the dragon because of its power and the force it could use against anyone who did not comply. Let's continue reading Revelation 13.

> *5 The beast was given a mouth to utter proud words and blasphemies and to exercise its authority for forty-two months.*

Again we come to this number: Forty-two months; 1260 days; three and a half; time, times and half a time. Each of these adds up to the same amount. For 1260 years the religious system the beast was using was allowed to exercise force against the people living in the parts of the world he could reach.

> **6 It opened its mouth to blaspheme God, and to slander his name and his dwelling place and those who live in heaven.**

Working through the beast, Satan spent that time slandering God's reputation. Remember that chapter 12, verse 9 translates five names for Satan—dragon, serpent, devil, adversary, deceiver. The Greek word for devil is *diabolos* which means slanderer. He led his followers to speak horrible things about God and what was happening in heaven, and even about the angels. He persuaded many that God would burn people forever and ever, and that people needed to ask saints to intercede for them with God instead of trusting Jesus who is our official mediator. Teaching people to believe that they are dependent on someone other than Jesus to forgive sins, and that Jesus is sacrificed again every time there is a communion service; teaching that even if Jesus loves us, God the Father hates us; that angels are little babies flying around after they have died here on earth, are some of the major ways that Satan and the beast have worked to tarnish and destroy God's reputation.

> **7 It was given power to wage war against God's holy people and to conquer them. And it was given authority over every tribe, people, language and nation.**
>
> **8 All inhabitants of the earth will worship the beast—all whose names have not been written in the Lamb's book of life, the Lamb who was slain from the creation of the world.**

God allowed the beast to have tremendous power. He was being fair to His worst enemy, allowing him to demonstrate what a world under his authority would be like. And most people went along with worshipping the beast, either because they believed what the beast said, or because they lived in fear of its power to destroy them.

How was the Lamb slain from the creation of the world? Long ago, the plan was made in heaven that Jesus would die for the sins of those on earth.

> 9. Whoever has ears, let them hear.
>
> 10. If anyone is to go into captivity,
>   into captivity they will go.
> If anyone is to be killed with the sword,
>   with the sword they will be killed.
>
> This calls for patient endurance and faithfulness on the part of God's people.

Verses nine and ten are saying, "Take warning!" to God's people. Very difficult times would come for them. They would need to be patient and faithful to Jesus as they endured lifetimes of danger and suffering. When we get to heaven, we can ask Jesus to explain to us why this time period needed to take place.

Revelation 13:11-18: The Beast from the Earth

> 11 Then I saw a second beast, coming out of the earth. It had two horns like a lamb, but it spoke like a dragon.

What is a lamb doing in the dragon's territory? Throughout the book of Revelation, it is a Lamb that defines God. This must be another attempt to imitate Jesus. But the imitation is only skin-deep because this lamb speaks like the dragon. The appearance is benign/gentle/innocent, but the reality is ominous. The message is different than you would expect from a lamb. Both the sea beast and the earth beast have forged identities. The wound of the first, and the lamb-like appearance of the second, are both intended to deceive.

Another perplexing detail here is that the lamb arises from the earth. The earth has so far been shown symbolically to be a good safe place. Now we find that here Satan will work deceptively, where it is least expected, to continue his warfare against God's people.

> 12 It exercised all the authority of the first beast on its behalf, and made the earth and its inhabitants worship the first beast, whose fatal wound had been healed.

This second beast is hand-in-glove with the first beast, forcing everyone to worship the sea beast. Because we know that the dragon is behind both of these beasts, we know that the three of them are in cahoots. They are promoting a conspiracy that they hope will take worship away from the real sovereign of the universe. God the Father, Jesus and the Holy Spirit have three enemies who are conspiring to imitate them.

> *13 And it performed great signs, even causing fire to come down from heaven to the earth in full view of the people.*

You remember the story from the Old Testament[22] where Elijah the prophet proposed the sign of fire from heaven as a way of determining the true God. Here in Revelation 13 the other side in the conflict appropriates this same miracle to show their power and establish their right to worship. This also reveals that the God of heaven no longer uses this miracle to prove His sovereignty.

> *14 Because of the signs it was given power to perform on behalf of the first beast, it deceived the inhabitants of the earth. It ordered them to set up an image in honor of the beast who was wounded by the sword and yet lived.*
>
> *15 The second beast was given power to give breath to the image of the first beast, so that the image could speak and cause all who refused to worship the image to be killed.*

The dragon gives power to the earth beast to give breath to the image of the first beast so it can speak. We usually think of images as inanimate objects that cannot speak, so this is another miracle performed by the earth beast. It reminds us of God breathing into Adam's nostrils the breath of life. (Genesis 2:7) So this ability is used by the dragon as further evidence of his power.

When the sea beast speaks, it is persuasive. People believe what it says. Nobody can be blamed for believing when the beast's power has been authenticated by miracles! When we consider more carefully, we find that its speech was deceptive. No wonder, because the ability to speak came from the dragon, who we know is a deceiver.

However, the beast added force to its persuasive speech.

---

[22] *1 Kings 18:20 and following verses.* 14

Fire from heaven, breath, and speech, used by the dragon, are all deceptive imitations of powers that belong to God. God only uses His power for the good of His people. But in verse 15 we read that the dragon and his side use their power to destroy people who refuse to worship them.

> *16 It also forced all people, great and small, rich and poor, free and slave, to receive a mark on their right hands or on their foreheads,*

Satan doesn't care whether people have a mark on their hands or on their foreheads. Hands represent doing whatever Satan says to do. Foreheads represent believing whatever he says.

Back in Revelation 7:3, during the intermission between the 6th and 7th seals, we read about the servants of God being sealed on their foreheads with the seal of God. Now we find that the other side also wants to put a mark on the hand OR the forehead of their followers. In the Old Testament in Deuteronomy 6 we read about the loving relationship with God that results from being sealed on the hand AND on the forehead.

> *5 Love the LORD your God with all your heart and with all your soul and with all your strength.*
>
> *6 These commandments that I give you today are to be on your hearts.*
>
> *7 Impress them on your children. Talk about them when you sit at home and when you walk along the road, when you lie down and when you get up.*
>
> *8 Tie them as symbols on your hands and bind them on your foreheads.*
>
> *9 Write them on the doorframes of your houses and on your gates.*

God's seal goes on our hands as well as our foreheads, because in a loving relationship, actions and thinking are in harmony. In the beginning of Revelation 14, we will find more evidence of the relationship those who are sealed will have with the Lamb and with God. They will have His name and His Father's name written on their foreheads. Now back to Revelation 13.

> *17 so that they could not buy or sell unless they had the mark, which is the name of the beast or the number of its name.*

There are economic benefits that come along with the mark of the beast. Accepting the mark indicates that a person worships the beast. By refusing to accept the mark, one faces not just economic hardship but the risk of death. No wonder that God's people are called to have patient endurance during such a time.

> *18 This calls for wisdom. Let the person who has insight calculate the number of the beast, for it is the number of a man. That number is 666.*

Remember that Revelation 1:1 alerted us to the fact that the book would be filled with symbols.

> *The revelation from Jesus Christ, which God gave him to show his servants what must soon take place. He made it known by sending his angel to his servant John.* **(emphasis supplied)**

Other versions of the Bible say "He signified it" which is a clearer translation, because the word "signified" means He used symbols. In verse 18 above, we find the word "number" used three times. It translates the Greek word "*arithmon*" or "*arithmos*." As you can see, the two words are almost the same, but they change a little bit because they are used as different parts of speech.

Back in Revelation 7:4, "*arithmon*" is used for the hundred and forty-four thousand which was a symbolic number for the redeemed. In Revelation 9:16, both "*arithmon*" and "*arithmos*" are used in relation to the army of two-hundred million, the symbolic number for the army on Satan's side. Finally in Revelation 20:8, "*arithmos*" is used of the lost who are like the sands of the sea.

We need to think carefully about the number of the beast. For ages, people have been trying to figure out to whom this is referring. In various languages, letters have number meanings. Because John wrote this book in Greek, should Greek letters and their number equivalents be used?

But a more important consideration is this: Does the call to "calculate the number" challenge us to use our arithmetic skill, or does it encourage us to use spiritual perception to get this right? Revelation has certainly given us lots of information to use in deciding which mark we choose to receive. Would you like to guess what the number would have been if it stood for perfection?

When the time comes that it is important for us to understand the meaning of the mark of the beast, we can be sure that God will guide our minds. The important thing now is for us to daily build our relationship with Jesus who has won the war and will shortly bring all things to an end.

After we summarize the symbols in chapter thirteen, we will turn our attention to chapter fourteen where we will read about how God reacts to what Satan is doing.

Symbols in Chapter Thirteen

- **The dragon goes away:** He adopts a new strategy of concealment rather than confrontation. He appears on the shore of the sea to call up his surrogate, the sea beast, who looks like him and does his bidding, leaving himself invisible in the background.
- **The sea:** The highly populated region toward the east end of the Mediterranean Sea and beyond. All the well-known history up to John's time had taken place in that area.
- **The different parts of the beast:** They refer to the characteristics of the beasts that Daniel saw come from the sea in Daniel 7.
   - A leopard—Greece brought rationalism and philosophy into their idol worship.
   - A bear—Medo-Persia merged various religions; covering all bases.
   - A lion—In Babylon, idolatrous religious power was stronger than political power.
- **Blasphemous name:** Each of the seven heads had something written on it that Satan hoped would ruin God's reputation.
- **Fatal wound:** an imitation of Jesus' death and resurrection to enhance the reputation of Satan's side and add to its power to deceive. The lives of anyone who tried to fight the beast were endangered. Only those who were faithful to Jesus would not worship the beast and the dragon.

- **The earth:** So far in the story the earth has worked on God's side. Now it is being usurped by Satan to add to his efforts to deceive. Compared to the sea, the earth was a less well-known part of the planet.

- **The lamb:** An imitation of Jesus. It starts out like a typical lamb, but don't be deceived. It metastasizes into a forceful power on the side of the sea beast and the dragon. The miracles it performs persuade or force people to choose between worshipping or being killed. Those who don't go along with its demands will lose the right to participate in the local economy as well as risk being killed.

- **Fire from heaven:** Imitation of the power God exhibited in the time of Elijah to prove who was the real God.

- **Breath:** Imitation of God's power to give life to a dead body.

- **Speech:** Reference to the snake in the garden of Eden who had the power of deceiving speech.

- **The image:** Like the three young men in Daniel 3, everyone will be required to worship something that the government sets up. Its power will be confirmed by miracles. Everyone will be required to show some kind of mark that they are cooperating.

- **Sealed on the hand:** Symbolizes a willingness to cooperate with laws even though the person may not agree with or believe in the laws.

- **Sealed on the forehead:** Symbolizes agreement based on being persuaded and believing in the law

- **The mark:**[23] An imitation of the seal of God to identify those who Satan claims are on his side with the beast in the cosmic conflict.

- **The number of his name:** A mysterious symbolic number; those who understand its meaning will have used their spiritual perception to interpret that it refers to something that reeks of incompleteness, and rejection of God's authority, and imperfection.

---

[23] *See the chart in Appendix A.*

CHAPTER 14
THE BIG PICTURE OF THE COSMIC CONFLICT, PART 3

In chapter twelve, which was Part 1 in the big picture of the cosmic conflict, we saw that there were three sections, but they were not in chronological order. Here again in chapter fourteen, we also find three sections that are not lined up chronologically. First is the triumphal celebration of victory in heaven. Remember that the book frequently reminds us what will finally happen. Lots of bad events are revealed in Revelation, but God wants us to always remember that everything is going to turn out all right. No, not just all right. Magnificently brilliantly triumphant. Actually, that celebration will happen last. So, we will cover it last.

Let's review how the three parts of the Big Picture of the Cosmic Conflict fit together. Chapter 12 is a bit like Daniel 2. Somewhat like the preview of history from Daniel's day to the end of time, Revelation 12 gives a sweeping overview of the whole controversy between Christ and Satan, starting in heaven before Creation. But then, like many other places in the Bible, Revelation enlarges on parts of the story. Chapter 13 enlarges on the behavior of Satan, the dragon, and reveals his plans for the future.

Jesus Wins! **121**

It ends with all God's people in danger of being killed. Because they are not willing to worship him, the devil judges God's people worthy of death. Now chapter 14 enlarges on Jesus' reaction to Satan's plans and reveals how He is going to win the war.

I believe chapter 14 will be easier to understand if we study the three parts in chronological order. So, we will begin with the three angels' messages in verses 6 through 13.

Revelation 14:6-13: The Three Angels' Messages

> *6 Then I saw another angel flying in midair, and he had the eternal gospel to proclaim to those who live on the earth—to every nation, tribe, language and people.*

The word gospel means good news. After all the sad things we have read about in Revelation, at last we have come to good news. And it is eternal, so that means it is always true. And it is for everyone on the earth, no matter who they are or where they live.

> *7 He said in a loud voice, "Fear God and give him glory, because the hour of his judgment has come. Worship him who made the heavens, the earth, the sea and the springs of water."*

The angel is saying this message in a loud voice so everyone can hear it. He is making it clear that this is very important news. To fear God does not mean to be afraid of Him. It means to reverence Him, to stand in awe of Him.

God's reaction to Satan's plans is to reveal that it is time for His judgment to take place. In response, all the people on His side in the conflict will reverence Him and give Him glory. It is very good news that He is in charge of judgment; not the devil!

And why is it that we worship Him? Because He is the Creator God. No other so-called gods have anywhere near that power. As usual, we can turn to the Old Testament to find this same message. **Psalm 96:5-13** gives us a wonderful background for the first angel's message.

> *5 For all the gods of the nations are idols: but the LORD made the heavens.*

> 6 Honor and majesty are before him: strength and beauty are in his sanctuary.
>
> 7 Give unto the LORD, O ye kindreds of the people, give unto the LORD glory and strength.
>
> 8 Give unto the LORD the glory due unto his name: bring an offering and come into his courts.
>
> 9 O worship the LORD in the beauty of holiness: fear before him, all the earth.
>
> 10 Say among the heathen that the LORD reigneth: the world also shall be established that it shall not be moved: he shall judge the people righteously.
>
> 11 Let the heavens rejoice, and let the earth be glad; let the sea roar, and the fulness thereof.
>
> 12 Let the field be joyful, and all that is therein: then shall all the trees of the wood rejoice
>
> 13 Before the LORD: for he cometh, for he cometh to judge the earth: he shall judge the world with righteousness, and the people with his truth.

Revelation 13 and 14 give contrasting messages[24]. In Revelation 13:6 we read that God's name and His dwelling were being slandered by the beast. How appropriate it is in 14:7 to find God's people are in awe of Him and speak well of Him.

In 13:8, we read that all the inhabitants of the earth would worship an idol. In 14:7, we are called to worship the Creator of the universe. In 13:16, the devil's final demand is that everyone be forced to receive a mark on their forehead or on their hand. In 14:7, God's hour has come. This is a critical moment in the history of the world. The great battle is coming to a climax.

There is another contrast here as well. Revelation 14:7 says to worship God who made heaven and earth, the sea, and the springs of water. In 8:10-11, during the time of the third trumpet, the blazing star that fell from heaven poisoned a third of the springs of water. What God made was poisoned by the devil.

---

[24] See the chart in Appendix A.

And we can't leave this verse without noting how similar it is to the fourth commandment in **Exodus 20:8-11**.

> 8 "Remember the Sabbath day by keeping it holy.
>
> 9 Six days you shall labor and do all your work,
>
> 10 but the seventh day is a sabbath to the LORD your God. On it you shall not do any work, neither you, nor your son or daughter, nor your male or female servant, nor your animals, nor any foreigner residing in your towns.
>
> 11 For in six days the LORD made the heavens and the earth, the sea, and all that is in them, but he rested on the seventh day. Therefore, the LORD blessed the Sabbath day and made it holy. (emphasis supplied)

Here is **Revelation 14:7** again so you can see the similarities close together.

> 7 He said in a loud voice, "Fear God and give him glory, because the hour of his judgment has come. Worship him who made the heavens, the earth, the sea and the springs of water." (emphasis supplied)

These two passages in the Bible have several words in common. The major difference is that Revelation 14 adds "the springs of water." Maybe that was just because God wanted us to see the contrast between what Satan did and what God did. Or maybe it was also because He wanted us to remember the flood story. See Genesis 7:11 and 8:2.

God's people living in the time of the First Angel will be worshipping Him on the seventh day and believing the story of the great flood that came in Noah's time. Jesus, as well as all the writers of the Bible, believed this story. Many people in the world today think that the flood story is just a myth, but we can look at the evidence in the rocks of the earth, take the word of Jesus and the Bible writers, and have confidence that it happened like Moses wrote about it in Genesis 6-9.

We are going to merely touch on the Second Angel's message, in Revelation 14:8, which announces the fall of Babylon. The opposition has collapsed in corruption and defeat. When we come to future chapters in Revelation, we will learn much more about Babylon the Great, so it is not necessary for us to spend more time on it now.

> *8 A second angel followed and said, "'Fallen! Fallen is Babylon the Great,' which made all the nations drink the maddening wine of her adulteries."*

Instead, we will move on to the Third Angel's message which is the longest of the three messages.

> *9 A third angel followed them and said in a loud voice: "If any one worships the beast and its image and receives its mark on their forehead or on their hand,*

This is a strong warning against worshiping a god instead of God and receiving the wrong mark instead of the seal of God. In fact, it is the most fearsome wording in the whole Bible.

> *10 they, too, will drink the wine of God's fury, which has been poured full strength into the cup of his wrath. They will be tormented with burning sulfur in the presence of the holy angels and of the Lamb.*

We need to think carefully about who causes what to happen in this very important verse. Do you remember what we learned about God's wrath? It is not like human wrath. In the Old Testament, in Hosea 11:7-8 we read about Ephraim, and it reveals to us what God's wrath and anger are like.

> *My people are determined to turn from me. Even though they call me God Most High, I will by no means exalt them. How can I give you up, Ephraim? How can I treat you like Admah? How can I make you like Zeboyim? My heart is changed within me;* all my compassion is aroused." **(emphasis supplied)**

Admah and Zeboyim were two small cities destroyed with Sodom and Gomorrah. When it says, "My heart is changed. . ." it uses a Hebrew word that means an inner earthquake. God is experiencing extremely strong emotions at the thought of losing Gentiles from small towns, or His people Israel—also called Ephraim, because his was one of the most important tribes. They are not emotions of anger as we know it, but of compassion. He loves and pities people who are determined to turn away from Him.

Hosea 12:14 gives us the end of the story.

> *"But Ephraim has aroused His bitter anger; his Lord will leave on him the guilt of his bloodshed and will repay him for his contempt."*

God, with great sadness, will finally allow Ephraim, and everyone else like him, to have the results of their bad choices. But it will not be God who sends the results. Remember that someone else is at work in this world. Also, remember that in the Old Testament, God graciously took responsibility for everything that happened, even though He did not cause the bad things.

Up to this time, we have found God restraining the power of the devil and his forces. You can review that in Revelation 7:1-3. During the Fifth Trumpet, we read which side was causing the destruction. In Revelation 9:11 we found: "They had as king over them the angel of the Abyss, whose name in Hebrew is *Abaddon* and in Greek is *Apollyon* (that is, Destroyer)."

In Revelation 9:5-6 we read which side tortures people, with some restraint from God. "They were not allowed to kill them but only to torture them for five months. And the agony they suffered was like that of the sting of a scorpion when it strikes. During those days people will seek death but will not find it; they will long to die, but death will elude them." Under the Sixth Trumpet, in Revelation 9:13-19, the restraint is taken away and the demonic forces are allowed to kill. Verse 18 reveals what happened: "A third of mankind was killed by the three plagues of fire, smoke and sulfur that came out of their mouths.

At the very end of time, during the Third Angel's Message, God will finally allow Satan full power to bring destruction on the earth. This is God's wrath "full strength" or unmixed. Remember the second half of Revelation 14:10: "They will be tormented with burning sulfur in the presence of the holy angels and of the Lamb."

Now we can understand who is doing what during the Third Angel's Message. God gives the strong warning, but it is the Satanic forces that torture people who are on their side. God's people are protected from that. The holy angels and the Lamb are witnesses to what happens, not the ones who are delivering the torture.

Verse 11 continues to reveal the awful consequences of being on the devil's side in the cosmic conflict.

> *11 And the smoke of their torment will rise for ever and ever. There will be no rest day or night for those who worship the beast and its image, or for anyone who receives the mark of its name."*

Now we can understand why God sent such a strong and scary message for John to write down for us. He was trying every way possible to help us realize the dreadful consequences of making the wrong choice at the end of time. Just like you see smoke rise up into the sky until it disappears, the smoke from the sulfurous fire that destroys Satan's followers will rise above the earth until it can no longer be seen.

Don't get worried about the phrase "for ever and ever." The little one-chapter book of Jude, just before Revelation, says that Sodom and Gomorrah suffered eternal fire. Verse 7: "In a similar way, Sodom and Gomorrah and the surrounding towns gave themselves up to sexual immorality and perversion. They serve as an example of those who suffer the punishment of eternal fire." Has anybody seen that fire lately? Of course not. It went out when everything had burned up that could burn.

But that is not the only consequence. "There will be no rest day or night for those. . ." Only God gives rest. "But the wicked are like the tossing sea, which cannot rest, whose waves cast up mire and mud." Isaiah 57:20.

In summary, this is the message of the Third Angel's warning in **Revelation 14** against accepting the mark of the beast:

> They will be tortured
>
> They will have no rest
>
> And why is that? Because they failed to heed the warnings against the one who instigates and orchestrates the torture.

> *12 This calls for patient endurance on the part of the people of God who keep His commands and remain faithful to Jesus.*

Those who believe in Jesus will be living through these difficult experiences, but they will be protected. Their wall of protection will be

God's way of life. By living in harmony with Him, they can receive all the blessings He wants to give them. However, they will be under great pressure from those who don't want to follow God's way. Then the verse says they will remain faithful to Jesus. Deeper study of the word "faithful" has revealed that it is not our faith that protects us. It is the faithfulness of Jesus. We will miss the mark if we try to depend on our faith. But Jesus gives us the gift of faith[25] and his faithfulness is always there for us.

A more accurate way to translate Revelation 14:12 is, "Here is a call for the perseverance of the believers, those who keep the commandments of God as revealed by the faithfulness of Jesus."

> *13 Then I heard a voice from heaven say, "Write this: Blessed are the dead who die in the Lord from now on."*
>
> *"Yes," says the Spirit, "they will rest from their labor, for their deeds will follow them."*

These people receive rest from God. Throughout the history of the world, God's people have faced many hardships. Just think of the persecution they faced in Egypt, and from Assyria and Babylon and Rome, and during the long 1260 days/years of persecution. Now at last they are living in the Good News era. Jesus is about to come the Second Time.

Revelation 14:14-20: The Harvest of the Earth

> *14 I looked, and there before me was a white cloud, and seated on the cloud was one like a son of man with a crown of gold on his head and a sharp sickle in his hand.*
>
> *15 Then another angel came out of the temple and called in a loud voice to him who was sitting on the cloud, "Take your sickle and reap, because the time to reap has come, for the harvest of the earth is ripe."*

Everyone on earth has made a final choice about which side to join. The actions of the dragon and his side in chapter 13, and the messages God has given in chapter 14 have led everyone to decide who to believe. Thus, the harvest of the earth is ripe. Some versions of the Bible translate it as "fully ripe."

---

[25] *Ephesians 2:8-9*

> *16 So he who was seated on the cloud swung his sickle over the earth, and the earth was harvested.*

At His Second Coming, Jesus Himself will raise to life those who are sleeping and will gather all His people like a harvest of grain. Our guardian angels will take us to join Jesus on the cloud to travel to heaven. So shall we ever be with our Lord Jesus!

> *17 Another angel came out of the temple in heaven, and he too had a sharp sickle.*
>
> *18 Still another angel, who had charge of the fire, came from the altar and called in a loud voice to him who had the sharp sickle, "Take your sharp sickle and gather the clusters of grapes from the earth's vine, because its grapes are ripe."*
>
> *19 The angel swung his sickle on the earth, gathered its grapes and threw them into the great winepress of God's wrath.*

It is worthwhile here to pause a moment and review again the meaning of the wrath of God. God loves us with an everlasting, unconditional love. But He also totally gives us freedom of choice. If the time comes that we have chosen not to live in harmony with Him, He regretfully leaves us to the consequences of our choice. He does not cause the bad things that happen as a result. In this Bible passage, the righteous have been taken to be with Jesus. The wicked are now at the total mercy of Satan—which is no mercy at all.

> *20 They were trampled in the winepress outside the city, and blood flowed out of the press, rising as high as the horses' bridles for a distance of 1,600 stadia.*

Now has come the end of time for those who did not choose to be on God's side. We understand that God's wrath is sadly giving them up to the consequences of their choices. Verse 20 does not say who trampled them, causing the blood to flow. Throughout the book of Revelation, Satan was the instigator of destruction. In later chapters we will read that people turned on their leaders and on each other, killing and being killed. Most likely, verse 20 is also a veiled reference to the fact that satanic forces are responsible for killing those who were not harvested as grain to be taken to heaven. The 1600 stadia was about 180 miles. Blood up to the bridles would be about five or six feet. It is hard to even think about such a flood of blood. But it shows us how horrible it is to be under the control of Satan.

1600 is a multiple of the number 4. In prophecy, the number 4 represents worldwide events—north, south, east and west. So that adds to this picture of the terrifying condition of the earth and its people at the end of time. There is every reason to be on Jesus' side in the Cosmic Conflict.

For an Old Testament reference, in Isaiah 63:1-5 is an implied prophecy of Jesus treading the winepress alone. He shed His blood for us, and He was alone. All His friends had left Him. Because He went through that experience, we do not have to go through that experience or be at the beck and call of Satan.

Revelation 14:1-5: The Victory Celebration

This part of our book is named, "The Cosmic Conflict from A to Z." At last, we have come to Z. This view is of the final event in the conflict. We can go back to the beginning of Revelation 14 and watch the glorious victory celebration. Remember that John is seeing events while standing at the open door to heaven, and as we read, we are there with him.

> *1 Then I looked, and there before me was the Lamb, standing on Mount Zion, and with him 144,000 who had his name and his Father's name written on their foreheads.*

This is taking place in heaven. Jesus the Lamb who was slain is there with 12 times 12,000 people who have all received the seal of God. They all have the name of Jesus and His Father, on their foreheads. It is the name of God as revealed by the Lamb who was killed with violence. Jesus has revealed to us what kind of God we love and serve. Remember, that the forehead means to believe and choose to accept what has been learned.

There are 12,000 for each of the tribes of Israel. This number symbolizes God's power and mercy in saving Israel as a whole, the complete family of God. Ephesians 3:6 says, "This mystery is that through the gospel the Gentiles are heirs together with Israel, members together of one body, and sharers together in the promise in Christ Jesus."

Jacob's twelve sons became the twelve tribes of Israel. Also, Jesus chose twelve disciples. Then God multiplies the small number by twelve thousand because everyone who chooses to be on God's side in the cosmic conflict is a part of spiritual Israel. If you need more evidence, here it is in Galatians 3:

> *26 So in Christ Jesus you are all children of God through faith,*
>
> *27 for all of you who were baptized into Christ have clothed yourselves with Christ.*
>
> *28 There is neither Jew nor Gentile, neither slave nor free, nor is there male and female, for you are all one in Christ Jesus.*
>
> *29 If you belong to Christ, then you are Abraham's seed, and heirs according to the promise.*

Let's read on in Revelation 14 to learn more about this crowd of happy people.

> *2 And I heard a sound from heaven like the roar of rushing waters and like a loud peal of thunder. The sound I heard was like that of harpists playing their harps.*

This celebration is a noisy one. The sounds of rushing water and thunder can drown out every other sound around you. Both of them can be very loud. But this celebration is also very musical. Can you imagine 144,000 people all playing harps at the same time? So, whichever of these sounds it is, it is coming from a happy occasion.

> *3 And they sang a new song before the throne and before the four living creatures and the elders. No one could learn the song except the 144,000 who had been redeemed from the earth.*

These people who lived through the final events on planet earth had an experience different from everyone else's. Therefore, they can sing a song about God's care that nobody else would understand.

> *4 These are those who did not defile themselves with women, for they remained virgins. They follow the Lamb*

> *wherever he goes. They were purchased from among mankind and offered as first fruits to God and the Lamb.*

Remember that a woman is a symbol for either the false or the true church. Symbolically these saints have not involved themselves with false doctrines. They have followed Jesus and His truth and bonded so tightly with Him that they will remain very close to Him even in heaven. They totally understand that their redemption is completely by the grace of God who has saved them. Nothing they did made them worthy to be saved. Because of what they endured, they have special positions in heaven.

> *5 No lie was found in their mouths; they are blameless.*

Just as they stayed away from false doctrines, they equally grew to be like Christ, because He changes them into His likeness. They obey all the commandments, not because they are trying hard to be obedient, but because Jesus died for them and is living in them. That leads them to love to do what He did and to be like Him. The Lamb that was slain is what they hang on to.

Before we leave Part IV, the Cosmic Conflict, we need to review the central place that chapter twelve plays in the book of Revelation. It is the summary of the whole controversy between Christ and Satan. Chapters thirteen and fourteen enlarge on that summary, but they don't take away from chapter 12's crucial role as the highpoint of Revelation's message to us. A good way to think of chapter twelve is as a very bright light that shines both backward and forward. It helps us to understand better what we read before it, and it enlightens us as to the meaning of the chapters that come afterwards. As we launch into Part V, the Seven Bowls, we will be guided and helped by what we have already learned. This is the value of re-reading Revelation.

Symbols in Chapter Fourteen

- **144,000:** is a number symbolizing God's power to save His whole family

- **Angels:** are God's messengers to bring us information and directions. Since Satan led one third of the angels to rebel against God, we need to look carefully to determine whether angels are good or bad

- **Women:** symbolize churches; churches have beliefs and teachings. We can carefully study the Bible and choose to believe only what it teaches

- **Gospel:** is a word that means good news; the good news is that Jesus has won the war, He has shown us what the Father is like, and He provides eternal life for everyone who chooses to be on His side in the cosmic conflict

- **Loud voice:** symbolizes how important the message is. It is for everyone, and it is loud enough and clear enough so nobody should be deceived. God would like to save everyone, but He always gives each person a free choice

- **God's hour has come:** Not long before Jesus was crucified, He said His hour had come (John 12:23). He was referring to His death on the cross. In Revelation 14, His hour is referring to the Second Coming which will soon take place. His hour is always a time of crisis, a time for a momentous event that marks a turning point in history.

- **Judgment:** is the time for reviewing evidence, and final decisions are made and announced about the consequences of each person's choices. Judgment is good news for everyone who is on God's side. It is a scary time for people who rebel against God and don't want to live in harmony with Him

- **Fear God:** This doesn't mean to be afraid of Him. It means to reverence Him, to stand in awe of Him. The better we become acquainted with Him, the more amazed we will be by how awesome He is.

- **The wine of God's fury, the cup of His wrath:** symbolize the final decision God has to make to abandon people to their fate. They have refused to respond to His love. He has done all He can to persuade them to be on His side. Finally, He has to sadly turn away and leave them. Each one is His child. He loves them and will miss them throughout eternity

- **Wine... poured out full strength:** symbolizes that God will finally remove all restraint on satanic forces. They are allowed to show what their side will do when God is not restraining them

- **The maddening wine of her adulteries:** symbolizes the false doctrines that confuse peoples' minds. "Her" refers to a church that has not been faithful to her husband, God. Instead, she has taught false beliefs that cause others to decide not to follow the truth about God

- **1600 stadia:** is literally equal to about 180 miles. "Up to the horses' bridles" would be about five to six feet deep. This is an unbelievable amount of blood. 1600 is also a multiple of the number 4 which stands for the whole world in prophecy, i.e., the four winds—north, south, east, and west. Once God has removed all restraints from Satan and his forces, every part of the earth will be thrown into violence and terror that is beyond conceiving. Let me just mention that in several stories in the Bible, the only safe place to be is on God's side (the flood, the Exodus from Egypt, Esther's story)

PART V
THE SEVEN BOWLS

After Chapters 12 and 13 and 14, which gave us the big picture of what has happened and what will happen, now we come to another group of seven. This time it will be Seven Bowls. We will see a major similarity to what happened in the last group of seven, the Seven Trumpets. It is helpful to think of chapters 12, 13 and 14 as a bridge between the Seven Trumpets and the Seven Bowls.

Remember that the Seven Trumpets were an exposé of satanic activity. Because they are so similar to what we will read now, we need to look carefully at the Seven Bowls to see if they show the same character as the Trumpets.

CHAPTER 15
OPEN HEAVEN

We are reminded again that the throne room in heaven with the elders and angels and four beasts around the throne is the command center for what is happening on earth. John is there at the open door, observing all that happens and writing it down for us to read. He understands that he is now seeing the final events of the great conflict that has been waged in the universe and on earth for thousands of years.

Revelation 15:1-4: Singing the Song of Moses, the Song Also Sung by the Lamb

> *1 I saw in heaven another great and marvelous sign: seven angels with the seven last plagues—last, because with them God's wrath is completed.*
>
> *2 And I saw what looked like a sea of glass glowing with fire and, standing beside the sea, those who had been victorious over the beast and its image and over the number of its name. They held harps given them by God*

Jesus Wins! **137**

> *3 and sang the song of God's servant Moses and of the Lamb:*
>
> *"Great and marvelous are your deeds,*
> *   Lord God Almighty.*
> *Just and true are your ways,*
> *   King of the nations.*
> *4 Who will not fear you, Lord,*
> *   and bring glory to your name?*
> *For you alone are holy.*
> *All nations will come*
> *   and worship before you,*
> *for your righteous acts have been revealed."*

Once again, as we have seen several times before, John begins with the end of the events, reassuring us that Jesus has won, and His people will soon triumph and be celebrating and praising Him in heaven. The song they sing has echoes from the Song of Moses in the Old Testament.

When the Israelites were safely across the Red Sea and their enemies were drowned and could never hurt them again, Moses wrote and sang a song, praising God for His miraculous deliverance. Then, just before he died, Moses was told by God (Deuteronomy 31:19) to write down another song and teach it to the Israelites to remind them of their covenant with God. And Moses also composed it for himself to remember the sin he committed by striking the rock instead of speaking to it. He was angry and he made it look to the Israelites like God was angry the same way he was. In that event, He did not honor God (Numbers 20:12) but in his song He testifies that God is the Rock and everything He does is good and right, even refusing to allow Moses to go into the promised land.

Here in Revelation, we find the redeemed singing the same kind of praise song to the Lamb who has rescued them from the sinful earth. They had expected God to work in their behalf, but they were surprised by what He chose to do. "Great and marvelous are your deeds" could rightly be translated, "Great and counter-intuitive are your deeds." They didn't expect God to do what He did. "... your righteous acts have been revealed" shows that the redeemed are amazed by how right God's acts have been.

Throughout the Bible we find people thinking that God should do something differently. Job, Habakkuk[18], the disciples[26], the saints under the altar, all have questioned God about what He was doing. Maybe you have questioned Him about something you did not think was fair or correct. I'm sure Joseph could not understand why he was headed to Egypt as a slave. I have sometimes had serious questions. At the end of time all our questions will have been answered, and we will praise God because it will be obvious that He always did exactly the right things, even though we were surprised by His actions.

Revelation 15:5-8: Readying the Seven Bowls

> *5 After this I looked, and I saw in heaven the temple—that is, the tabernacle of the covenant law—and it was opened.*

This reminds us of both the tabernacle tent built out in the desert at Sinai and Solomon's beautiful temple in Jerusalem. Each of them was designed as a pattern of a temple in heaven.[27] The tabernacle of the covenant law was a name for the golden ark of the covenant that was kept in the Most Holy Place. It contained the two tables of stone on which God had written the ten commandments with His own finger. The shekinah glory shown from its cover because it was symbolically God's throne. No one except the High Priest could ever see this ark. And even the High Priest could only go into the room one time each year when He appeared before God as the people's representative.

When Jesus died, the inner veil that separated the Holy Place from the Most Holy Place was torn from top to bottom.[28] This could not have been done by a human being because the embroidered curtain was extremely heavy. "The rending of this curtain signified that the old order of ceremonies and sacrifices in an earthly sanctuary was over. It also began a new era when people could approach God directly through Christ in the heavenly sanctuary (Heb 10:19-22).[29]

> *6 Out of the temple came the seven angels with the seven plagues. They were dressed in clean, shining linen and wore golden sashes around their chests.*

---

[26] *Mark 8:31-33*
[27] *Exodus 25:40 and Hebrews 8:5*
[28] *Matthew 27:51*
[29] *Andrews Study Bible NIV on Matthew 27:51*

> *7 Then one of the four living creatures gave to the seven angels seven golden bowls filled with the wrath of God, who lives for ever and ever.*

Notice that the bowls are handed to the angels by one of the four living creatures who, we remember, stand around the throne of God. There is certainly no surprise in heaven that these things are happening. There is no panic. Heaven is prepared for what is coming next. God has ultimate control over events, even if He is not the one who performs the events.

Also, we should remember that this is an open heaven. God does not have secrets He doesn't want us to know. He wants us to understand. That is the reason He sent John the vision and told him to write the book.

> *8 And the temple was filled with smoke from the glory of God and from his power, and no one could enter the temple until the seven plagues of the seven angels were completed.*

In the Old Testament, we find examples of this happening. In Exodus 40:34-35 we read that when Moses had finished setting up the tabernacle and all was in readiness for its services to begin, "Then the cloud covered the tent of meeting, and the glory of the Lord filled the tabernacle. Moses could not enter the tent of meeting because the cloud had settled on it, and the glory of the Lord filled the tabernacle."

Again, in 2 Chronicles 5:13-14 when Solomon's temple was completed and the dedication service had already begun, ". . . Then the temple of the Lord was filled with the cloud. And the priests could not perform their service because of the cloud, for the glory of the Lord filled the temple of God." I Kings 8:10-11 has almost the same words. In each of these stories, it was the glory of God's presence being in the temple in such a powerful way that made it impossible for humans to enter. In the Old Testament it is referred to as a cloud. Here in Revelation fifteen, it is described as smoke. To the human eye, a cloud and smoke look similar.

Both of these stories tell of the end of one phase—preparation—and the beginning of the next phase—God in His place, guiding His people. In Revelation, the empty temple signals the close of human probation, which will soon be followed by the beginning of God's eternal kingdom of glory. Remember that God gave the pattern used for the temples on earth because He wanted to dwell with His people. We can be sure that while there is silence in heaven, God is still very close to His children. And, the Holy Spirit is still very close to each of God's children who are anxiously waiting on earth for their rescue and redemption.

And this brings us to the end of this short chapter. Now we will turn to chapter sixteen to learn about each of the bowls and what they contain.

Symbols in Chapter Fifteen

- **Seven last plagues:** This is a further enlargement of chapter 14, where the somber warning was given about the results of choosing to be on the side of the dragon and his minions. The last plagues will be the details about the results of not choosing to be on Christ's side in the conflict. They are the last, because God is no longer restricting the devil's actions. He is now allowed to show exactly what a world governed by him is like. The devil's personal destruction will follow.

- **A sea of glass is in heaven before God's throne.** See Revelation 4:6

- **The victorious are shown in heaven**, even though they are actually still on earth waiting for their rescue. This shows that the triumph of the people of God is near and sure.

- **The temple, that is, the tabernacle of the covenant law:** This is the name of the open ark of the covenant revealing the 10 commandments, pointing us to our relationship with God whose character of love is reflected in His holy law.

- **The empty temple:** is so filled with God's glorious presence that no one else can enter until the mysterious work of the seven last plagues is finished.

CHAPTER 16
SEVEN BOWLS OF WRATH

Revelation 16 contains all the Bowls. We will find they are very similar to the Seven Trumpets. Let's review what those were like.

Were the trumpets good events or bad events? They were bad events that got worse and worse. Who was causing those bad events? We studied that they were caused by satanic action. The trumpets were an exposé of Satan's activity.

Chapter 12 showed clearly that there are two actors in this world: Christ and Satan. Christ works by way of truth and freedom of choice. Satan works by way of deception and force.

At the end of Revelation 15 we read about an empty temple. No more intercession for sin will be taking place. This indicates that probation had closed. Everyone has made their final choice. Only the last events on this sinful world will still have to take place.

Now that we come to the Seven Bowls, we will need to pay close attention to see in what ways they are like the Seven Trumpets. We have seen already that heaven is deeply involved. Something terrifying happened in the trumpets. Something worse is going to happen in the bowls, but who is doing it?

Just to review, what major help did we use to interpret the seven trumpets? How can that continue to help us as we study the bowls?

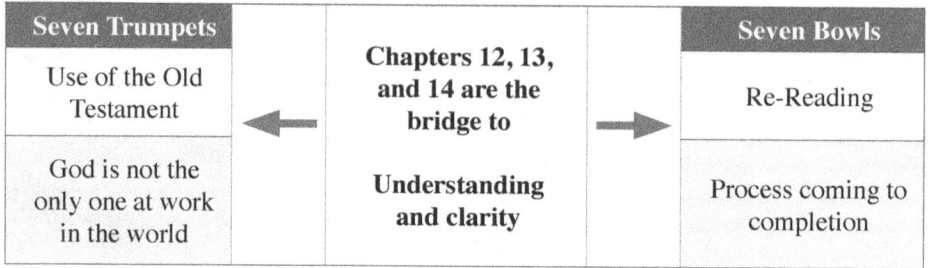

Seven Trumpets	Chapters 12, 13, and 14 are the bridge to	Seven Bowls
Use of the Old Testament		Re-Reading
God is not the only one at work in the world	Understanding and clarity	Process coming to completion

The trumpets in Revelation 8 and 9 were an exposé of satanic activity. Now we read that the seven bowls are God's wrath poured out on the earth. What is God's wrath? Remember that it is not at all like human wrath. It is what happens when God sadly leaves people to the consequences of their own bad choices. God told Moses how this would happen.

Deuteronomy 31

> *17 And in that day I will become angry with them and forsake them; I will hide my face from them, and they will be destroyed. Many disasters and calamities will come on them, and in that day they will ask, 'Have not these disasters come on us because our God is not with us?'*
>
> *18 And I will certainly hide my face in that day because of all their wickedness in turning to other gods.* (emphasis supplied)

When Moses wrote this, he was referring to times during the judges and the Babylonian captivity when God removed this protection because of His peoples' sins. In addition, when you read "that day" in the Bible, it is referring to Christ's Second Coming. In these verses we see that God's anger near the time of the Second Coming also results in people being forsaken by Him. He hides His face, and disasters come because they have chosen to follow other gods, and they finally realize that the true God is no longer with them. It specifically is not saying that God causes the disasters. They come from a different source.

To summarize, the Seven Bowls are major ecological disasters that result when God removes His protecting hand from those on the earth who choose not to side with Him. Day by day we are dependent on God for health and healing and protection. After probation closes, those of us on God's side will continue to receive constant care and attention from God. Remember from chapter 15 that God is still in the temple, even though the usual ministry is not going on. But those who have chosen to rebel against God will suddenly lose all the dependable blessings and stability that they had taken for granted would continue on the earth. The results are horrifying, as we will see.

Revelation 16:1-9: The First Four Bowls

> *1 Then I heard a loud voice from the temple saying to the seven angels, "Go, pour out the seven bowls of God's wrath on the earth."*
>
> *2 The first angel went and poured out his bowl on the land, and ugly, festering sores broke out on the people who had the mark of the beast and worshiped its image.*

Before we continue through the Bowls, we should look at something else that happens when we compare the seals, the trumpets and the bowls.

Bad	Worse	Worst
Seven Seals	Seven Trumpets	Seven Bowls
A fourth of the earth (Revelation 6:8)	One-third of the earth and the sea (Revelation 8:7-8)	Every living thing in the sea died (Revelation 16:3)

As we progress through the seals and the trumpets and the bowls, everything goes from bad to worse. Also remember that the one-third mentioned so many times in the trumpets is not just quantity, it is also indicating who is causing the trouble.

After God removes His protection and the first bowl is poured out, it is the human body that is afflicted. Various times people have pointed to a newly discovered disease as one of the final plagues. But because the close of probation has not yet taken place, nobody yet has the mark of the beast and the seven last plagues have not begun. Unfortunately, when probation does close, the first plague will be an even worse disease than any before.

> *3 The second angel poured out his bowl on the sea, and it turned into blood like that of a dead person, and every living thing in the sea died.*

Can you imagine? No more possibility for people to earn their living from fishing. No more fish in the sea for anyone to enjoy looking at or eat. No more cruise ships carrying people through beautiful blue waters. No more clouds of mist rising from the seas to fall as rain on the earth.

> *4 The third angel poured out his bowl on the rivers and springs of water, and they became blood.*

After the seas become blood, all the rest of the sources of water also turn to blood. Where in the world can people get the water they need for washing and cooking and drinking? We use water all day long for one purpose or another. What would we do without it?

> *5 Then I heard the angel in charge of the waters say:*
>
> *"You are just in these judgments, O Holy One,*
>   *you who are and who were;*
>
> *6 for they have shed the blood of your holy people and your prophets,*
>   *and you have given them blood to drink as they deserve."*
>
> *7 And I heard the altar respond:*
>
> *"Yes, Lord God Almighty,*
>   *true and just are your judgments."*

An angel voices his approval that God has allowed this judgment because it is appropriate in light of the blood shed by the martyrs and prophets who have been killed down through the ages. Probably more martyrs will be dying just before the seven bowls are poured out.

The altar responds. Altars are inanimate objects that can't speak. This has to be a symbol. Throughout Old Testament times, millions and millions of animals were sacrificed on the altar as reminders that the true Lamb of God was coming to redeem His people. Once Jesus had died on the cross, sacrificing animals had no more spiritual significance. Here the altar shows us that the time is over for martyrs to shed their blood. Once probation has closed, there will be no more reason for God's people to be killed. Their death would not be able to convince anyone to be on God's side.

> 8 The fourth angel poured out his bowl on the sun, and the sun was allowed to scorch people with fire.
>
> 9 They were seared by the intense heat and they cursed the name of God, who had control over these plagues, but they refused to repent and glorify him.

The fourth bowl is poured out on the sun, and scorching heat is the result. People curse God and blame Him for the heat when they should be blaming Satan who is showing what kind of a world he can deliver. The plagues do not result in anyone repenting or speaking well of God.

Trumpets and Bowls Compared		
	TRUMPETS	**BOWLS**
1	Hail, fire, and blood fall on the **earth**	The bowl is poured on the **earth**
2	A blazing mountain falls into the **sea** One third of the sea becomes **blood** A third of **sea creatures die**	The bowl is poured on the **seas** The seas become **blood** Every living thing in them **dies**
3	A blazing star falls on a third of **rivers and fountains of water**	The bowl is poured on **rivers and fountains of water**
4	A third of **sun**, moon, and stars are struck, **resulting in darkness**	The bowl is poured on the **sun**, resulting in fierce heat

We can see how closely the first four bowls match the first four trumpets. It was clear that a demonic force was at work in the world during the time of the trumpets. Who do you think is at work in these terrible scenes during the bowl sequence?

Revelation 16:10-16: The Fifth and Sixth Bowls

> *10 The fifth angel poured out his bowl on the throne of the beast, and its kingdom was plunged into darkness. People gnawed their tongues in agony*
>
> *11 and cursed the God of heaven because of their pains and their sores, but they refused to repent of what they had done. (emphasis supplied)*

This time the bowl is poured out on the throne of the beast, the heart of Satan's empire. Compare that with the fifth trumpet in Revelation 9:1-2:

> *1 The fifth angel sounded his trumpet, and I saw a star that had fallen from the sky to the earth. The star was given the key to the shaft of the Abyss.*
>
> *2 When he opened the Abyss, smoke rose from it like the smoke from a gigantic furnace. The sun and sky were darkened by the smoke from the Abyss.*

We learned when we studied the trumpets that the star that fell was Lucifer, the rebellious angel who was driven out of heaven. And we saw that the smoke from the Abyss was what caused the darkness. In the trumpets, Satan's throne is the bottomless pit. In the bowls it is called the throne of the beast.

	Trumpets and Bowls Compared	
	TRUMPETS	**BOWLS**
5	Shaft of the **bottomless pit** opened. Sun and moon are **darkened** by smoke Locusts **torture** people	The bowl is poured out on the **throne of the beast** Plunging it into **darkness** People bit their tongues in **severe pain**

6	The four angels bound at **the great river Euphrates** are released **Cavalry** numbering two hundred million **kills a third** of humankind	The bowl is poured on **the great river Euphrates** Kings of the world **assemble for battle** on the great day of God the Almighty at the place called **Armageddon**
7	**Loud voices in Heaven** Announce the coming of the kingdom of God and Christ	The bowl is poured into the air **A loud voice from the throne** announces, "It is done"

Look at each of the parallels that are in bold print. A demonic force was at work in the world during the Seven Trumpets. We see similar things on the Bowl side. What does this show? Except for the loud voice(s) at the time of the 7th trumpet and 7th Bowl, from heaven and from the throne, who is responsible for the action that is taking place?

Coming to the sixth bowl, here is a map showing the geographic location of the river Euphrates. It can remind us of several different stories in the Old Testament. Because it is a large river, crossing it with an army was always a major hurdle.

The Sixth Bowl

> *12 The sixth angel poured out his bowl on the great river Euphrates, and its water was dried up to prepare the way for the kings from the East.*
>
> *13 Then I saw three impure spirits that looked like frogs; they came out of the mouth of the dragon, out of the mouth of the beast and out of the mouth of the false prophet.*
>
> *14 They are demonic spirits that perform signs, and they go out to the kings of the whole world, to gather them for the battle on the great day of God Almighty.*

In the table below we can look more closely at the similarities between the sixth trumpet and the sixth bowl.

Climactic Scenes at the River Euphrates	
TRUMPETS	**BOWLS**
• Then the sixth angel blew his trumpet. . ."Release the four angels who are bound at the great river Euphrates" (9:14)	• The sixth angel poured out his bowl on the great river Euphrates (16:12)
• The number of the mounted troops was [two hundred million]. I heard their number.	• They are demonic spirits that perform signs, and they go out to the kings of the whole world, to gather them for the battle on the great day of God Almighty (16:14)
• The power of the horses was in their mouths and in their tails; for their tails were like snakes, having heads with which they inflict injury (9:19)	• And I saw coming from the mouth of the dragon, and from the mouth of the beast, and from the mouth of the false prophet three unclean spirits like frogs (16:13)

We can see that both the Sixth Trumpet and the Sixth Bowl have to do with the great river Euphrates and preparation for a major battle. Up to that point in time, there was restraint on them, but they were released from that restraint at the time of the Sixth Trumpet. In the Sixth Bowl they are clearly not restrained any more. This is what happens at the end of time, what the book of Revelation calls the wrath of God coming to completion. Both scenarios feature mouths.

We learned that the Sixth Trumpet revealed satanic action, and now in the Sixth Bowl we are told specifically that the players are demonic spirits. Both the trumpets and the bowls reveal deceptive speech and readiness for war. Demonic spirits are now allowed to play out their strengths without restraint.

If you look up the word Armageddon on the computer, you will find that there are many millions of references to it. It has truly become a major legacy word from the book of Revelation. Lots of people are studying and thinking about it. What it is; where it is; when and how will the battle happen?

In Isaiah 45:1, Cyrus was predicted as a type of Jesus the Messiah. He came from the east to overthrow ancient Babylon and deliver Israel from the Babylonian captivity. Christ will also come from the east to deliver His people from end-time Babylon at the battle of Armageddon. Just like God's people of old left Babylon to return to Jerusalem, so God's people will leave the earthly spiritual Babylon to enter the new Jerusalem.[30] In the ancient event, there was no need to fight a battle and all God's people were saved. At the end of time when Christ comes, there will be no need to fight, and all God's people will be delivered from this earth and taken to heaven.

To review, we see demonic forces at work and coming to completion in the trumpets. In the bowls we see the exact same events described with no restraint on them. So, faced with these parallels, what does this show?

> 15 "Look, I come like a thief! Blessed is the one who stays awake and remains clothed, so as not to go naked and be shamefully exposed."

A thief surprises people who are not guarding their house from invasion. Christ's coming is not like a thief for those of us who are prepared and expecting Him. We are blessed if we are alert to what is happening in the world, seeing that it is almost time for Jesus to come. We remain clothed by being covered with His righteousness. That protects us from the harm around us in this world and keeps us ready to rejoice at His coming.

> 16 Then they gathered the kings together to the place that in Hebrew is called Armageddon.

Revelation 16:17-21: The Seventh Bowl

> 17 The seventh angel poured out his bowl into the air, and out of the temple came a loud voice from the throne, saying, "It is done!"

When Jesus died on the cross, the last thing He said was, "It is finish." His sacrifice for sin was complete. Here at the time of the Seventh Bowl, a loud voice from the throne of God says, "It is done!" The thousands of years of sin have come to their last moments. All that God has done to convince the universe of His fairness and love has finally come to completion. It is over, it is done. The risk He ran in giving freedom of choice to those

---

[30] *Andrews Bible Commentary, Old Testament, page 1029*

He created has been worthwhile. He wanted to share His love with those who could love Him back. He didn't want to fill the universe with lots of robots who could be programmed to do whatever He said.

> *18 Then there came flashes of lightning, rumblings, peals of thunder and a severe earthquake. No earthquake like it has ever occurred since mankind has been on earth, so tremendous was the quake.*

We have read similar verses in Revelation 4:5 concerning the throne of God, in 8:5 at the time of the seventh seal, and in 11:19 at the time of the seventh trumpet. Remember repetition and enlargement. These are all descriptions of the same earthquake. They are echoes of God's appearance on Mt. Sinai. Each time these events indicate that a revelation is in progress. And this time it is coming to completion.

> *19 The great city split into three parts, and the cities of the nations collapsed. God remembered Babylon the Great and gave her the cup filled with the wine of the fury of his wrath.*

The earthquake will be so powerful that buildings, no matter how strongly built, will not be able to withstand it. All of this is happening because rebellion against God finally leads Him to leave people and their things to the consequences of choosing Satan's side in the cosmic conflict.

> *20 Every island fled away and the mountains could not be found.*

We read a similar expression in Revelation 6:14 near the end of the seals. The whole cosmic order is in some ways disintegrating. Except that it is not covered with water, the earth is returning, more or less, to the state it was in before creation. Creation was reversed at the time of Noah's flood. Again, at the end of time, creation will be mostly reversed. Satan wanted to totally control the earth. Now is his chance to show what "his" earth will look like. Even though God still maintains control over these plagues (See verse 9), He allows Satan to show what he can do.

> *21 From the sky huge hailstones, each weighing about a hundred pounds, fell on people. And they cursed God on*

account of the plague of hail, because the plague was so terrible.

The reaction of people to this horrible plague is to blame God. There is no indication that any one of them would want to change sides in the conflict. It is too late for them to realize that the only safe place to be is on Jesus' side. This is what the third angel in Revelation 14 had warned them.

Symbols in Chapter Sixteen

We have already reviewed God's wrath so many times that it is not necessary to discuss that again. Sores, the sea, rivers and springs, the sun. the throne of the beast, the river Euphrates, and the earthquake are the focuses of the seven late plagues. It is impossible to know how literal or how symbolic these will be until they actually happen. What we can know for sure is that these will be terrible events that bring great destruction and suffering on those who choose to be marked on Satan's side rather than be sealed on Jesus's side.

Under God's control, conditions of nature have been mostly dependable. In Genesis 8:22, after the flood, God promised, "As long as the earth endures, seedtime and harvest, cold and heat, summer and winter, day and night will never cease." In general, He has fulfilled that promise.

In the last few years. we have seen climate and weather patterns changing. Also, we know from history that at times, smoke and ash from large volcanoes have cooled the earth for long enough that crops did not mature in certain years. There have been periods of drought or too much rain, but in general, the earth has remained stable until now. People have taken for granted that this was just natural. They have not realized that it was God controlling events.

During the final plagues, God will have withdrawn His protection. Satan will be totally in charge of the earth. It will be seen just how inadequate and corrupt his administration of earth can be.

At the same time, God's people will be miraculously protected from all the terrible things happening on the earth. Those experiencing the plagues will see that God's people are safe. Although it will be an intense time of

CHAPTER 16   Seven Bowls Of Wrath

mental anguish and life-threatening hostility, the godly will be surrounded by angels who protect them from the physical, geographic, and atmospheric destruction that will be happening all around them.

Now we will turn to Revelation 17 and find a complex mystery! Fortunately, one of the angels who poured out a bowl will guide us through the strange symbols.

PART VI
REVELATION
17 THROUGH 18

Remember that the Bible often tells something, then tells about it again with more details—repetition and enlargement. It is repetition because we already know in general about the topic. It is enlargement, because now we get more details about the topic. God uses this repetition to add to our knowledge and to assure us of important things that will definitely happen. In chapter twelve, we had the big picture of the cosmic conflict between Christ and Satan and how it affects Christ's people.

Chapter seventeen that we are about to read is another example of repetition and enlargement. It expands the information about the cosmic conflict revealed in chapter twelve. But first it gives the surprising meaning of the wicked woman.

Chapter eighteen tells the story of fallen Babylon. Then we will come to the last chapters of Revelation that are good news for those on God's side.

CHAPTER 17
THE BEAST THAT WAS, AND IS NOT, AND IS TO COME

Let's look at a summary of chapter seventeen before we begin reading it. One of the bowl angels invited John to come with him so he could see what would happen to a particular wicked woman. They traveled where they could view the woman and John was astonished to find out about her. He saw where she was, how she was dressed, what she had done and what names she had. She was seated on a beast.

The angel asked John why he was astonished and said he would explain all about the woman and the beast she was sitting on. And for the rest of the chapter, the angel does just that. He goes through one detail after another, telling John—and us—just what they mean.

So now that we have had that preview, we are ready to begin reading the chapter.

Revelation 17:1-7: The Angel Shows John the Great Prostitute

> *1 One of the seven angels who had the seven bowls came and said to me, "Come, I will show you the punishment of the great prostitute, who sits by many waters.*

We are not told which angel will be John's guide, but one of the bowl angels summons him—and us—to see what will happen in the future to the person he calls the great prostitute. Quite likely it could be the sixth bowl angel, because that bowl was poured out on the river Euphrates which flowed through the city of Babylon, and here we will learn more about Babylon. This woman sits by many waters, so we can expect to learn what that means as well.

> *2 With her the kings of the earth committed adultery, and the inhabitants of the earth were intoxicated with the wine of her adulteries."*

The prostitute is obviously someone who has lots of influence on the political leaders in the world. She has made them drunk. When people are drunk, they have lost their ability to think clearly and rationally. Back in Revelation 14:8 we read that Babylon the great was forcing all the nations to drink the maddening wine of her adulteries. Maybe there is some connection between Babylon the great and this prostitute since both of them are using "the wine of her adulteries."

> *3 Then the angel carried me away in the Spirit into a wilderness. There I saw a woman sitting on a scarlet beast that was covered with blasphemous names and had seven heads and ten horns.*

Notice that the scarlet beast was covered with blasphemous names. That means the beast was saying wrong things about God, because blasphemy means the act or offense of speaking sacrilegiously about God or sacred things.

The last time we read about a woman in the wilderness, she was the woman who had given birth to the baby the dragon was trying to kill as soon as he was born. Her child was snatched up to God and to his throne (Revelation 12:5). Then the dragon went after the woman, and she was removed to the wilderness for her protection (verses 13, 14).

> *4 The woman was dressed in purple and scarlet, and was glittering with gold, precious stones and pearls. She held a golden cup in her hand, filled with abominable things and the filth of her adulteries.*

The first half of this verse portrays the woman dressed in the same color as the beast she is sitting on. The purple and scarlet colors of her dress are images of royalty, but also of worldliness. They have a prestigious connotation and also a negative connotation. The second half of the verse clarifies that her dress is associated with bad things, not good things.

> *5 The name written on her forehead was a mystery:*
> *BABYLON THE GREAT*
> *THE MOTHER OF PROSTITUTES*
> *AND OF THE ABOMINATIONS OF THE EARTH.*

The fact that she is called the mother of prostitutes can refer to the fact that she is the first one, or it could mean that she is the worst one.

> *6 I saw that the woman was drunk with the blood of God's holy people, the blood of those who bore testimony to Jesus. When I saw her, I was greatly astonished.*

No wonder John is astonished! There could hardly be a greater difference between the righteous woman in chapter twelve who was given eagles' wings to fly into the wilderness for protection and now this one. Yet, apparently, they may be the same woman. Over time, it seems the woman has changed sides in the cosmic conflict. John was horrified. He was expecting to see a woman by many waters. Instead, he sees this "fancy" woman sitting on a very strange beast. How could this possibly be? Remember that a woman in the Bible represents the church.

Revelation 17:8-18: The Angel Explains the Beast and the Woman

> *7 Then the angel said to me: "Why are you astonished? I will explain to you the mystery of the woman and of the beast she rides, which has the seven heads and ten horns.*

In Revelation 12:3 the enormous red dragon had seven heads and ten horns. In Revelation 13:1 the beast coming out of the sea had seven heads and ten horns. And that beast was the front man for the dragon who wished to change his tactics and be invisible. Remember that the phrase "went away" in chapter 12:17 actually means he disappeared. You can see the value of re-reading because there are complex relationships among the different parts of the book of Revelation.

In chapter twelve the dragon is the star that fell from heaven and brought one-third of the angels with him. He stands before the woman who is about to give birth. He is defeated in his designs on that woman. Later in chapter twelve the dragon is pursuing the woman who is still God's believing community.

Here in chapter 17, we also find a woman, a wilderness and an abnormal animal. The dragon in chapter 12 and the sea beast in chapter 17 seem to look the same, but the woman has changed.

- In chapter 12 she was fleeing for protection from the dragon. In chapter 17 she is cooperating with him.
- In chapter 12 she was being persecuted. Now in chapter 17 she is the one doing the persecuting. She is drunk with the blood of the saints.
- In chapter 12 she was a God-fearing faithful woman. In chapter 17 she is a prostitute.

No wonder John was horrified! But the angel is going to explain this mystery.

> 8 *The beast, which you saw, once was, now is not, and yet will come up out of the Abyss and go to its destruction. The inhabitants of the earth whose names have not been written in the book of life from the creation of the world will be astonished when they see the beast, because it once was, now is not, and yet will come.*

God is described in Revelation 1:4, 8 and in chapter 4:8 as "He who is and who was and who is to come." God is always present in the past, in the present and in the future. We know from re-reading Isaiah 14:14 that Satan wants to make himself like God.

Also, Jesus died for us, and then was resurrected and returned to heaven to be our intermediary. Satan is trying to imitate Jesus and get the same power He has, to be like God. Since he has temporarily disappeared, it can be said of him that he once was and now is not. But he has plans to come back in greater strength. Although most people will be very impressed when he does return, those who have their names written in the Book of Life will not be influenced by him.

> *9 "This calls for a mind with wisdom. The seven heads are seven hills on which the woman sits.*

Here we come to information that is for intelligent people. We must think very carefully about this. Here is where chapter seventeen gets a lot more complex. The angel's explanation now turns from the woman to the character of the beast she is sitting on.

> *10 They are also seven kings. Five have fallen, one is, the other has not yet come; but when he does come, he must remain for only a little while.*
>
> *11 The beast who once was, and now is not, is an eighth king. He belongs to the seven and is going to his destruction.*

First, we need to figure out who this beast is. Three times we read that he once was, and now is not. Two times it added that he will come again, and two times it also added that he will go to his destruction. Verse 8 gives us the final clue we need to know who the beast is. It says he will come up out of the Abyss. Several other versions of the Bible use the phrase "the bottomless pit" instead of "Abyss."

In Revelation 9:1, 2 we read that there was a star that fell from heaven and was given the key to the Abyss or the bottomless pit. That became his location, his address, his headquarters here on earth. From there he launched his terrible attacks on a third of this and a third of that, reminding us that his tail had brought down a third of the stars or angels from heaven. In verse 11 of that chapter, we read that the king of the Abyss is an angel, and his name is Destroyer in Greek and Hebrew and English.

So, put together all these clues:

- **He fell from heaven**
- **he is the king of the Abyss**

- he is an angel
- his name is Destroyer
- he blasphemously says wrong things about God
- he was and is not
- he will come up out of the Abyss
- and is going to his destruction

An Old Testament text for his destruction is Isaiah 14:20, the last verse of the description of Satan that begins in verse 12: "you will not join them in burial, for you have destroyed your land and killed your people." Satan's horrible character as a destroyer ensures that he himself will be destroyed at the end. He has orchestrated destruction all the time that he has been the prince of this world, the title he stole from Adam. That is why the verse called it "your land" and "your people."

This beast can be none other than the devil himself. The beast the woman rides on is Satan. And there is more evidence. In Revelation 11:7 the beast that comes from the Abyss attacked and killed the two witnesses. In chapter 20 we will discover that Satan's key to the Abyss was a spare key, and not the master key, because an angel will come down from heaven with a key to the Abyss and lock up Satan the dragon. There can be no doubt that he is the one who resides there.

Now let's turn our attention to what John's angel guide says about the seven heads. The seven heads are seven hills (or seven different locations). They are also seven kings (or kingdoms) and there will be a related eighth. So, this cannot be seven literal hills. Seven is the symbolic number for completeness. We will repeat verse 10 and 11 so we can think about them carefully.

The one The other

> *10 They are also seven kings. Five have fallen, one is, the other has not yet come; but when he does come, he must remain for only a little while.*

The first five hills/kings are lumped together. Of more interest are the next two, the one and the other. The one (number 6) is now. The other (number 7) has not come. Remember these are heads of the beast that we have identified as Satan. Numbers 6 and 7 are heads of a **beast** who **isn't** the sea beast and **isn't** the earth beast. So, it seems logical that those **heads ARE** the sea beast and the earth beast. Did you get that? They are heads on the beast that we know is Satan. So, head number 6, the one that is now, is the sea beast. Head number 7, the other that will remain for only a little while is the earth beast. The sea beast is the one who looks like the dragon and stands in for him while he is invisible. The earth beast forces everyone to worship the sea beast and the dragon. They all work together. Here the sea beast and the earth beast have been reduced to heads on the dragon. It is good news that when the 7th king does come, he must remain for only a little while.

> *11 The beast who once was, and now is not, is an eighth king. He belongs to the seven and is going to his destruction.*

The eighth king is now easy to identify because we have already talked about the fact that he once was, and is now invisible, and he is going to his destruction. The eighth king is none other than Satan himself. Of course he belongs to the seven. He is their body. They are his heads.

Now let's think about the first five heads that are lumped together. Obviously, because they are some of his heads, they are entities that worked together with Satan promoting his misrepresentation of God.

Notice that here we are not reviewing the history of the world, such as Daniel 2 showed. Here we are just thinking about the activities of the heads of the beast. Think about which kingdoms had power over God's people to persecute them through the many years before Jesus came to die and be resurrected. It was at that point that Satan chose to disappear and use a front man, the sea beast, to carry out his orders.

- **Egypt**
- **Assyria**
- **Babylon**
- **Greece**
- **Rome**

All of these kingdoms persecuted God's people. Do you notice that one kingdom was left out? Medo-Persia did not generally persecute God's people. Cyrus was named by God many years before he was born. He was referred to as anointed (messiah) and shepherd, the same names that are used for Jesus. He let the Jews return home to Jerusalem and he provided help for building their temple.³¹ The Darius who was king when Daniel was put into the den of lions was on Daniel's side and probably became a God worshiper.³² We may meet him in heaven. Later, Darius the Great again helped the Jews and provided all they needed to finish building the temple.³³ God saved His people from wicked Haman in the time of Queen Esther, and the Persian king participated in that rescue. The next king, Artaxerxes, helped Ezra go to Jerusalem to rebuild the city and establish the government there.³⁴ Later he also sent Nehemiah to rebuild the walls of Jerusalem and again provided support and help.³⁵

We really don't know about much persecution during the time that Persia was the dominant power—except for the crisis involving Queen Esther. God's people still had trouble, because the surrounding neighbors such as the Horonites, Ammonites, and Arabs, and even some inside Jerusalem, harassed them,³⁶ but the king of Persia always sided with them and helped them out.

> *12 "The ten horns you saw are ten kings who have not yet received a kingdom, but who for one hour will receive authority as kings along with the beast.*
>
> *13 They have one purpose and will give their power and authority to the beast.*

These ten horns are political powers that will come together at the end of time to fight in unity with Satan and his forces. They have one purpose, which is to give their power and authority to the beast. That time will be short as evidenced by the fact that it is only for one hour.

> *14 They will wage war against the Lamb, but the Lamb will triumph over them because He is Lord of lords and King of kings—and with Him will be His called, chosen and faithful followers."*

They will not be able to defeat the Lamb. Jesus has already won the war because He is Lord of lords and King of kings. This will just be the last battle. May each one of us be among his called, chosen and faithful followers!

---

[31] *Isaiah 44:28; 45:1-5, 13*
[32] *Daniel 6*
[33] *Ezra 5:3-17; 6:1-15*
[34] *Ezra 7:11-26*
[35] *Nehemiah 2:1-9*
[36] *Nehemiah 2:10, 19; Nehemiah 3; Nehemiah 6:1-14*

> **15** *Then the angel said to me, "The waters you saw, where the prostitute sits, are peoples, multitudes, nations and languages.*

Way back at the very beginning of chapter seventeen, in the first verse, John's angel guide refers to the woman who sits by many waters. Finally, now, he is going to reveal what that means. The many waters are peoples, multitudes, nations and languages. In other words, the woman is influential in crowded cities and places where there are lots of people.

> **16** *The beast and the ten horns you saw will hate the prostitute. They will bring her to ruin and leave her naked; they will eat her flesh and burn her with fire.*

Now the angel discloses what will ultimately happen to the woman. God is not going to destroy her. The people, the rulers, those who were led into sin by her, will turn on her. They will hate her and destroy her. Because she was a symbol of the church, she can be related to the religious systems in the Old Testament. If the daughter of a priest in Israel became sinful, she was to be burned, not stoned to death.[33] This is further evidence that this woman is a religious power.

> **17** *For God has put it into their hearts to accomplish his purpose by agreeing to hand over to the beast their royal authority, until God's words are fulfilled.*

Now we see something amazing. Those ten powers thought they were fulfilling the beast's purpose, but here we read that they were actually accomplishing God's purpose when they handed over to the beast their royal authority. God was in control the whole time. He was working out the best way to end the cosmic conflict.

> **18** *The woman you saw is the great city that rules over the kings of the earth."*[34]

---

[37] *See Leviticus 21:9*

[38] *"The Lord wants His people to follow other methods than that of condemning wrong, even though the condemnation be just. He wants us to do something more than to hurl at our adversaries charges that only drive them further from the truth. The work which Christ came to do in our world was not to erect barriers and constantly thrust upon the people the fact that they were wrong . . . The very last work in the controversy may be the enlightenment of those who have not rejected light and evidence, but who have been in midnight darkness and have in ignorance worked against the truth. Therefore, treat every man as honest. Speak no word, do no deed, that will confirm any in unbelief" (6T 121, 122)*

We should not jump to the conclusion that this refers to one specific great city. It can be any big place that blasphemes God, combining church and state to promote the dragon's misrepresentation of the truth and control the minds of people.

In 1 Kings 18 we read about Queen Jezebel of the northern kingdom of Israel killing prophets.

> *13 Haven't you heard, my lord, what I did while Jezebel was killing the prophets of the LORD? I hid a hundred of the LORD's prophets in two caves, fifty in each, and supplied them with food and water.*

In Luke 13 we read Jesus' words that Jerusalem was the city where prophets were killed.

> *34 "Jerusalem, Jerusalem, you who kill the prophets and stone those sent to you, how often I have longed to gather your children together, as a hen gathers her chicks under her wings, and you were not willing.*

We can also think of other places we have heard of where people lose their freedom of choice and are persecuted for their religious beliefs.

Symbols in Chapter Seventeen

As we have followed the Apostle John and his angel guide through this chapter, we have received very clear explanations for each symbol. If you still have questions, I suggest you reread the chapter, because each symbol can only be interpreted in relation to other verses that go along with it and make it understandable.

CHAPTER 18
BABYLON'S FALL

This chapter is a continuation of the narrative in chapter seventeen. There the main subject was the wealthy wicked woman. In this chapter, the subject is a wealthy wicked city. Beginning in Genesis, cities were always associated with wickedness. In the Old Testament the Jews were taken captive to the land of Babylon whose capital city had been known for centuries as the center for pagan worship.

We have read about this city before. Revelation 14:8 tells us for the first time that, "Fallen, fallen, is Babylon the Great which made all the nations drink of the maddening wine of her adulteries." In Revelation 16:19 the great city split into three parts when God gave her the cup filled with the wine of the fury of his wrath. We know by now that means God had to abandon her to the consequences of her choices. In Revelation 17:3-5 we found that Babylon the Great is the mother of prostitutes, reinforcing the idea that adultery is a chief sin of Babylon. And adultery is a symbol of false ideas about God. The mother of prostitutes can mean the first one, or it can also mean the worst one. She has been a spiritual entity, combining spiritual ideas with government power, as an instrument to promote the dragon's misrepresentation of God.

Revelation 18:1-3: Lament Over Fallen Babylon

Here in Revelation 18, John's expanded vision of Babylon the Great continues.

> *1 After this I saw another angel coming down from heaven. He had great authority, and the earth was illuminated by his splendor.*

Another angel comes who is so bright and glorious that he lights up the whole earth. We see that God delegates great authority to His angel messengers. This angel proclaims a description of the city's demonic character.

> *2 With a mighty voice he shouted:*
>
> *"'Fallen! Fallen is Babylon the Great!'*
> *She has become a dwelling for demons*
> *and a haunt for every impure spirit,*
> *a haunt for every unclean bird,*
> *a haunt for every unclean and detestable animal.*
> *3 For all the nations have drunk*
> *the maddening wine of her adulteries.*
> *The kings of the earth committed adultery with her,*
> *and the merchants of the earth grew rich from her excessive luxuries."*

In Revelation 14:8 we read the same message in brief. The language comes from Isaiah 21:9 and Jeremiah 51:8 in the Old Testament. Jeremiah tells us that God wanted to heal Babylon, but she didn't choose to be healed. God's people should leave her and return to Judea. That is another piece of evidence that God wants to save everyone, but when individuals or nations choose to reject Him, He has no option but to leave them to the consequences of their choices.

In this chapter, the message about the city of Babylon is enlarged. The angel is describing a supposedly spiritual city filled with impure, unclean, and detestable inhabitants. She has used adultery as a way to influence and engage with "all the nations." This is a strong indictment that what is wrong with her is mostly what Satan has said about God, which she has promoted to the nations. This means that what she has said about God is what has led to her downfall. In addition, massive luxuries have made her popular with those who clambered to sell her their luxurious products. So, Babylon represents a combination of economic, political and religious forces used in demonic ways.

Revelation 18:4-8: Warning to Escape Babylon's Judgment

Next, we hear another voice's warning to escape Babylon's judgment. Terrible things will soon happen to her. Everyone should get away from her, so they don't participate in her judgment.

In Numbers 16:23-25 you can read the story of Korah, Dathan and Abiram who rebelled against God's plan for only Aaron and his descendants to have the priesthood. The rest of the Levites had other responsibilities for the temple and its work. God told Moses to warn the Israelites to get away from those three rebellious men. Moses urged everyone to move back and not touch anything that belonged to them.

Here in Revelation, as Babylon is facing judgment, God sends a final warning to everyone to come out of her so they will not have the same fate she is facing. And we will find that even the kings of the earth, and the merchants, and the sea-faring people will stand far off from her. This is the final call for people to separate from any entity that does not chose to be on God's side.

> *4 Then I heard another voice from heaven say:*
>
> *"'Come out of her, my people,'*
> *so that you will not share in her sins,*
> *so that you will not receive any of her plagues;*

And now the angel describes her judgment where we see that the punishment fits the crimes. We must be careful when we think about who it is that is tormenting her. We are plainly told that God in heaven is paying attention to what is going on. He knows all about her crimes. We are not plainly told who it is that executes the punishment. Remember the meaning of God's wrath. Who will give back? Who will send plagues on her?

> *5 for her sins are piled up to heaven,*
> *and God has remembered her crimes.*

> 6 Give back to her as she has given;
>   pay her back double for what she has done.
>   Pour her a double portion from her own cup.
> 7 Give her as much torment and grief
>   as the glory and luxury she gave herself.
> In her heart she boasts,
>   "I sit enthroned as queen.
> I am not a widow;
>   I will never mourn."
> 8 Therefore in one day her plagues will overtake her:
>   death, mourning and famine.
> She will be consumed by fire,
>   for mighty is the Lord God who judges her.

God is the one who judges her, but in Revelation 17:16 we discovered who it is that burns her up. It is not God, it is the beast and the ten horn kings.

In Revelation 14:8 we read that Babylon the Great had fallen. She was the one who made all nations drink the maddening wine of her adulteries. In the very next verse, we read about the grave danger of being associated with her. Here in chapter 18, we are finding out more about her fall and its consequences.

In Jeremiah 51:35, 36, 50, God warned his people, through Jeremiah's preaching, to flee from the actual city of Babylon. When their seventy years of exile ended, many of them were tempted to stay there instead of returning to Jerusalem. Now in Revelation we read God's warning to flee from the spiritual city of Babylon.

Revelation 18: 9-20: Threefold Woe Over Babylon's Fall

Next, we will read about the three groups who are lamenting Babylon's downfall. They stand far off and pronounce woes on her, as they worry about what will now happen to them. It sounds like they aren't really sorry to see her go, they are just sorry to lose the benefits they used to get from her and are terrified that they might have to share her fate. First the kings of the earth, then the merchants of the earth, and finally the seagoing community all decry her destruction because of what it means they will be losing.

9 "When the kings of the earth who committed adultery with her and shared her luxury see the smoke of her burning, they will weep and mourn over her.

10 Terrified at her torment, they will stand far off and cry:

*"'Woe! Woe to you, great city,
   you mighty city of Babylon!
In one hour your doom has come!'*

11 "The merchants of the earth will weep and mourn over her because no one buys their cargoes anymore—

12 cargoes of gold, silver, precious stones and pearls; fine linen, purple, silk and scarlet cloth; every sort of citron wood, and articles of every kind made of ivory, costly wood, bronze, iron and marble;

13 cargoes of cinnamon and spice, of incense, myrrh and frankincense, of wine and olive oil, of fine flour and wheat; cattle and sheep; horses and carriages; and human beings sold as slaves.

Notice that in addition to lovely luxurious items, they also deal in animals and human beings with all the suffering and anguish included in that business. Several places in the Bible refer to God's care for animals. In addition, any culture that has practiced slave trading comes under this indictment.

Ezekiel 28:12-16 reveals the cosmic extent of this passage and helps us understand Revelation 18. The guardian cherub was definitely not a human being. He was created perfect and beautiful beyond compare. Then he became wicked. Verse 16 talks about his widespread trade. Verse 18 calls it his dishonest trade. What trade did Lucifer engage in? His aim was to destroy God's reputation, so his trade was slander, lies and inuendo about God. Verses 17 – 19 tell the rest of his story. Pride for his beauty and splendor corrupted him and led to his sinfulness. Ultimately, he was expelled from his position beside the throne of God, and then thrown out of heaven, down to the earth. You and I and all human beings and even nature are still dealing with him at this time. At the very end, fire comes out of him and destroys him, leaving only ashes on the ground.

Isaiah 14:2-20 is the other passage in the Old Testament that reveals the story of Lucifer who became Satan. John weaves these two passages together in writing Revelation.

Now, reading on about the city that will also come to its end:

> 14 "They will say, 'The fruit you longed for is gone from you. All your luxury and splendor have vanished, never to be recovered.'
>
> 15 The merchants who sold these things and gained their wealth from her will stand far off, terrified at her torment. They will weep and mourn
>
> 16 and cry out:
>
> "'Woe! Woe to you, great city,
>   dressed in fine linen, purple and scarlet,
>   and glittering with gold, precious stones and pearls!
>
> 17 In one hour such great wealth has been brought to ruin!"
>
> Every sea captain, and all who travel by ship, the sailors, and all who earn their living from the sea, will stand far off.
>
> 18 When they see the smoke of her burning, they will exclaim, "Was there ever a city like this great city?"
>
> 19 They will throw dust on their heads, and with weeping and mourning cry out:
>
> "'Woe! Woe to you, great city,
>   where all who had ships on the sea
>   became rich through her wealth!
> In one hour she has been brought to ruin!"

> 20 Rejoice over her, you heavens!
> Rejoice, you people of God!
> Rejoice, apostles and prophets!
> For God has judged her
> with the judgment she imposed on you.

We see at the close of this section that the people of God will rejoice that Babylon has fallen, because through the years she had persecuted them just like the actual city of Babylon had persecuted the Jewish exiles. When she is gone, they are safe, and they see that her judgment is fair, because she will have gotten back what she gave to others. By judging her, God has saved them.

Revelation 18:21-24: The Silent City

In the final section of this chapter, an angel throws a huge stone into the sea and states in many ways that Babylon is finished. She will never show up again. Never is the word he uses over and over. She has become a silent ghost town.

> 21 Then a mighty angel picked up a boulder the size of a large millstone and threw it into the sea, and said:
>
> "With such violence
> the great city of Babylon will be thrown down,
> never to be found again.
> 22 The music of harpists and musicians, pipers and trumpeters,
> will never be heard in you again.
> No worker of any trade
> will ever be found in you again.
> The sound of a millstone
> will never be heard in you again.
> 23 The light of a lamp
> will never shine in you again.
> The voice of bridegroom and bride
> will never be heard in you again.

Some of the same wording was used about Jerusalem at the time of the Babylonian Captivity. Jeremiah 16:9 says: "For this is what the LORD Almighty, the God of Israel, says: Before your eyes and in your days I will bring an end to the sounds of joy and gladness and to the voices of bride and bridegroom in this place." And in Jeremiah 25:10 it says: "I will banish from them the sounds of joy and gladness, the voices of bride and bridegroom, the sound of millstones and the light of the lamp."

However, there is a big difference. In Revelation the silence in Babylon would never, never, never change. In Jeremiah's prediction about Jerusalem, the end result would be different. Read the next verse in Jeremiah 25: "This whole country will become a desolate wasteland, and these nations will serve the king of Babylon seventy years." And that was exactly what happened. God arranged events so that God's people were back in Jerusalem and the country of Judea just at the end of the seventy years. We can be very confident that God has arranged events now so that the prophecy about Babylon also comes to pass.

Continuing in Revelation 18:

> *23 Your merchants were the world's important people*
> *By your magic spell all the nations were led astray.*

Why did this judgment come upon Babylon the Great? How did she lead all the nations astray? Most magic is simple tricks that anyone who wants to can learn to do, but some magic is only performed by a connection with satanic powers. We have already learned that Babylon has been a front man to promote Satan's lies about God. In the final verse of this chapter, we find that Satan's lies have not just deceived most of the people of the world into believing slander about God, but as a result, they have been led to persecute God's people who refused to side with them.

> *24 In her was found the blood of prophets and of*
> *God's holy people,*
> *of all who have been slaughtered on the earth."*

God sees everything that is going on. He knows what Satan is trying to do. Satan wants to kill everyone who refuses to be on his side and receive his mark. Remember, from Isaiah 14:13, 14, Satan is trying to be like God, maybe even take God's place. But God is far more powerful than Satan. He will protect and save His faithful people who are willing to die rather than believe or spread a lie about Him. They have seen through Satan's magic and his false doctrines and want nothing to do with his side in this cosmic controversy. The final line of the chapter is proof that Babylon the Great is not just one city. This is a cosmic crisis that started in heaven. It is all the cities and organizations through time who have persecuted those who remain true to God.

Babylon is undone as a failed spiritual entity because its faith and power were used to promote Satan's misrepresentation of God. Babylon is a failed economic entity because it was oppressive and unsustainable. Babylon is undone as a cosmic reality, because the covering cherub and his trade in slander and slaughter come to an end. Jesus wins! Why did God allow Satan so much time? Because God deals in truth and openness. He gives freedom of choice to each human being and wants everyone's questions to be answered.

In many parts of the world, throughout history, Satan has inspired people and organizations and governments to persecute and kill God's faithful people. All of these are included in Babylon the Great, whose time has come for complete destruction.

Symbols in Chapter Eighteen

- **Babylon the Great:** a symbol of false religion, of persecution of anyone who disagrees with her, of opposition to God throughout history

PART VII
REVELATION
19 THROUGH 22

Remember that Jewish minds in Bible times wanted to hear the end of the story first. Then they were prepared to think about the events leading up to the end. Before Revelation 15 told of the seven last plagues, in verses 2-4, it gave a magnificent view of God's people gathered in heaven, praising Him for great and marvelous deeds, His just and true ways, His holiness, and His righteous acts. Only after this reminder did John write about the fearful last plagues.

Here again in Part VII, Chapter 19, we find a jump to the end of the story. Despite all the horrible events that are happening at the end of time on this earth, God wants to remind us that He is in control and the glorious finish will soon come. His people will then understand and applaud the way He handled the awful crisis of sin.

In chapter 20 we will read of the end of sin, followed by two chapters describing the wonderful plans God has for his family after sin is gone forever.

Jesus Wins! 177

CHAPTER 19
A HUGE CELEBRATION

Revelation 19:1-10: Victory Is Celebrated in Heaven with a Wedding

1 After this I heard what sounded like the roar of a great multitude in heaven shouting:

"Hallelujah!
Salvation and glory and power belong to our God,
2 for true and just are his judgments.
*   He has condemned the great prostitute*
*   who corrupted the earth by her adulteries.*
He has avenged on her the blood of his servants."

3 And again they shouted:

"Hallelujah!
The smoke from her goes up for ever and ever."

Jesus Wins! **179**

"Her" is Babylon. This is the same wording as in Revelation 14:11 And we see that this is happening in the heavenly council, just as we saw in Revelation 5:8. Throughout the intervening chapters, all the action has played out in the presence of this group of twenty-four elders on thrones and four living creatures around the throne of the throne of God and of the Lamb who had been slain.

> 4 The twenty-four elders and the four living creatures fell down and worshiped God, who was seated on the throne. And they cried:
>
> "Amen, Hallelujah!"
>
> 5 Then a voice came from the throne, saying:
>
> "Praise our God,
> all you his servants,
> you who fear him,
> both great and small!"

One of the living creatures around the throne is a choir director who leads the praise service. All the participants speak well of God, praising Him for what He has done and is doing. Their voices are joined by those of millions of angels and the saved of all ages.

> 6 Then I heard what sounded like a great multitude, like the roar of rushing waters and like loud peals of thunder, shouting:
>
> "Hallelujah!
> For our Lord God Almighty reigns.
> 7 Let us rejoice and be glad
> and give him glory!
> For the wedding of the Lamb has come,
> and his bride has made herself ready.
> 8 Fine linen, bright and clean,
> was given her to wear."
>
> (Fine linen stands for the righteous acts of God's holy people.)

> *9 Then the angel said to me, "Write this: Blessed are those who are invited to the wedding supper of the Lamb!" And he added, "These are the true words of God."*

The story that began in Genesis 3 with distrust of God ends here in a marriage where trust has been restored. In this marriage at the end, the relationship and circumstances exceed that of the marriage in the Garden of Eden. That marriage and break-up focused on the humans involved. This one at the end focuses on a relationship with God. This one is a true affair of the heart. The Lamb loves the bride. He has sacrificed himself for her. The bride loves, honors, and identifies with the Lamb. She has thought about and planned for and prepared herself for this wedding.

You and I have the infinite privilege of being invited to this wedding!

> *10 At this I fell at his feet to worship him. But he said to me, "Don't do that! I am a fellow servant with you and with your brothers and sisters who hold to the testimony of Jesus. Worship God! For it is the Spirit of prophecy who bears testimony to Jesus."*

In Deuteronomy 18:15, 18, Moses testified about the coming of Jesus the Messiah who would be the ultimate witness. He would be a prophet who would teach people the truth about God. Jesus Himself affirmed this prophecy in Luke 24:27, "And beginning at Moses and all the prophets, he expounded unto them in all the scriptures the things concerning himself."

When Philip talked to Nathanael, he showed that he understood this prophecy to refer to Jesus. (John 1:45)

Peter, in Acts 3 healed a lame beggar then preached a powerful sermon showing that Jesus was the Messiah predicted by Moses. God had sent the Messiah to bless them with omnipotent truth.

As Stephen preached to the Jews just before they stoned him, he also testified that Jesus was not only the one Moses predicted, He was also the God who was with them in the wilderness. Moses had received from Him "living words" to pass on to the Israelites.

So, what can we say about the Testimony of Jesus? It is His words of truth from His own mouth, and those handed down to us from Him through prophets. He has not left us alone and lonely. He has provided comfort and direction and instruction and wisdom for us as we wait for His Second Coming. We can be sure He is paying close attention to us and is interested in everything that is happening to us.

Revelation 19:11-16: The Last War--Armageddon

> *11 I saw heaven standing open and there before me was a white horse, whose rider is called Faithful and True. With justice he judges and wages war.*
>
> *12 His eyes are like blazing fire, and on his head are many crowns. He has a name written on him that no one knows but he himself.*

This Rider is Revelation's last glorious picture of Jesus before the cosmic conflict is over. It centers on the name that no one knows. It is God's name, because He is the Word of God, and it is Revelation's mission to reveal it.

> *13 He is dressed in a robe dipped in blood, and his name is the Word of God.*

In Revelation 6:1-2, we also saw a rider on a white horse, but what a difference! That rider was armed for war with a bow as a weapon. He went out intent on conquering. This rider has a robe dipped in blood because He died for us, and He is the Word of God. He is defined by the robe He wears. Both of them are revealed by the weapons they carry.

> *14 The armies of heaven were following him, riding on white horses and dressed in fine linen, white and clean.*
>
> *15 Coming out of his mouth is a sharp sword with which to strike down the nations. "He will rule them with an iron scepter." He treads the winepress of the fury of the wrath of God Almighty.*

In revealing what God is truly like, He carries only truth. His weapon is truthful words. The iron scepter is the symbol of His authority because He has won the war, He is the King.

We know what the wrath of God is. Jesus takes responsibility for dealing with those who did not choose to be on His side. You will see what happens in the next chapter.

> *16 On his robe and on his thigh he has this name written:*
> **KING OF KINGS AND LORD OF LORD**

As we read on, we find that a different supper is being served. This is one we would not want to be a part of.

Revelation 19:17-21: A Picture of Wastelands

> *17 And I saw an angel standing in the sun, who cried in a loud voice to all the birds flying in midair, "Come, gather together for the great supper of God,*
>
> *18 so that you may eat the flesh of kings, generals, and the mighty, of horses and their riders, and the flesh of all people, free and slave, great and small."*

This is a depiction of an army that has come to grief. They have been defeated, and they are eaten by vultures. There is no one to bury them.

> *19 Then I saw the beast and the kings of the earth and their armies gathered together to wage war against the rider on the horse and his army.*

In Revelation 16:12-16, we saw the unclean spirits who were going out TO gather the kings of the whole world for the battle on the great day of God Almighty. Here in Revelation 19, they ARE gathered to wage war against the rider on the horse and his army. This is the battle, and we can see who won.

> *20 But the beast was captured, and with it the false prophet who had performed the signs on its behalf. With these signs he had deluded those who had received the mark of the beast and worshiped its image. The two of them were thrown alive into the fiery lake of burning sulfur.*

Who captured the beast? Not the Rider on the horse. Those who the beast had deceived and who had received the mark of the beast are now undeceived and very vengeful. Chaos reigns in the camp of the deceiver. The beast and the false prophet are thrown into a fiery lake. Then the rest turn on each other as they seek out who they can blame for their being deceived. They kill each other, but it is because of the sword of truth and witness that they finally understand when it is too late to be healed by it.

> **21 The rest were killed by the sword coming out of the mouth of the rider on the horse, and all the birds gorged themselves on their flesh.**

This final view in chapter nineteen is clearly a revelation of what will take place. It is not a scene of retribution where God is punishing humans for their sins. It is further evidence of what happens when the devil is allowed to be fully in charge of those he has deceived.

CHAPTER 20
THE THOUSAND YEARS

The Apostle John who was seeing this vision wanted to make sure we understood that a thousand years is involved in this part of the story, so he included it six times, in verses 2 and 3 and 4 and 5 and 6 and 7. From God's viewpoint, a thousand years is like only one day. But from a human viewpoint, a thousand years is a very long time. So, let's see what we can learn about what God intended for John to teach us about this time period, and what it teaches us about Jesus.

As John wrote this, he brought in strong connections to Revelation 12. Satan is defined as the dragon, the ancient serpent, and the devil in both places. And when he is called the ancient serpent, it is to remind us that the story started in Genesis 3 when the serpent deceived Eve and drew both Adam and Eve onto his side in the cosmic conflict. It was also the time that Jesus made His first promise to save us. At last, now, we come almost to the end of this long and difficult story of the cosmic conflict.

Jesus Wins! **185**

CHAPTER 20   The Thousand Years

Revelation 20:1-3: Satan Bound for a Thousand Years

This ending to the story of sin brings big questions to our minds. Why in the world was Satan bound instead of being destroyed? Why was he allowed to exist and cause trouble, mayhem, chaos and grief for such a long time? Why was he allowed to tell lies about God? Isn't God powerful enough to put a stop to that? You may have thought of other questions. As we go through this chapter, we will be looking for answers.

> *1 And I saw an angel coming down out of heaven, having the key to the Abyss and holding in his hand a great chain.*
>
> *2 He seized the dragon, that ancient serpent, who is the devil, or Satan, and bound him for a* thousand years.
>
> *3 He threw him into the Abyss, and locked and sealed it over him, to keep him from deceiving the nations anymore until the* thousand years *were ended. After that, he must be set free for a short time. (emphasis supplied)*

Why must Satan be set free? We have heard of people who were put into prison for crimes they did not commit. It is right that they be released. But the evidence against Satan is more than strong. It is overwhelming. Why would he be allowed out to commit more crimes? To answer these questions, we must review what we know about the whole cosmic controversy.

Lucifer, the highest angel in heaven, the choir director, the beautiful one next to God's throne, decided he deserved worship as much as God did. (Isaiah 14:12-14). From his high position he had lots of influence on other angels and even on other planets throughout the universe. When he began a smear campaign against God, many angels and inhabitants of other places were willing to listen to what he had to say.

Ultimately, he persuaded one third of the angels to follow him, resulting in their being forced out of heaven down to this newly created earth. No longer referred to as Lucifer (Light-Bearer), he became known as Satan (accuser or adversary). Other places in the universe didn't agree with his complaints, but they were not totally sure whether or not he was right. Remember He was a master deceiver. Later, when he killed his Creator, they had their questions all answered and they rejected everything he had told them.

What would have happened if God had handled the problem a different way? What if God had wiped out Satan as soon as he began to question? That would have raised more questions and doubts in the minds of those who had loved and followed Lucifer. So, God, in His infinite love and fairness, allowed Satan to show his true colors down through time until everyone's questions are answered, and minds are settled into God's truth, instead of Satan's lies.

Before we continue thinking about the questions we have, let's turn our attention to what we have just read in verses 1-3 about what this angel did. We find the following strong verbs:

Angel coming down

He seized

and bound

and threw

and locked

and sealed (20:2-3a)

These verbs impress upon us that Satan is an important figure in this story. Also, he is a non-human. He is not God; he is not man. He is an angel. As in any good story, we expect that the ending will be related to the beginning. Satan the serpent comes into the story in the third chapter of the Bible. Now we are finding the end to his story in the third chapter from the close of the Bible.

We have noted before that John sometimes uses hyperbole as part of his symbolic language. In verses 2 and 3 we can understand that it was circumstances that John is talking about that contain the devil, not literal locking up with a chain.

At Christ's second coming, all the righteous leave this earth to go to heaven. All the other people die. Satan and his angels are confined to only this earth because they have lost all sympathy from anyone else in the universe. They are not welcome anywhere else. So, for a thousand years they sit on a destroyed earth with nobody to harass or tempt into sin. Think of it as sitting in the corner for all that time. If one of your parents ever gave you timeout to sit in the corner, what did they want you to do there? To do nothing except think about what it was you had been doing wrong.

Freedom of choice is very important to God. Jesus died so each one of us could have freedom of choice. Rebellion doesn't come to an end until every person, and every creature in the universe, has made a final choice and had their questions answered. Satan's release serves as a final demonstration of the character of sin and its consequences.

Since Satan wants to take God's place, he has done his best to convince the whole universe that God is selfish, unfair, and arbitrary. God has responded by thousands of years of evidence that He is not like that. He is love. He is full of pity for our sorrows and difficulties. He sacrificed His son Jesus who came to earth and became a human being in order to show us what God is like. When Jesus died, the rest of the universe had their questions answered and were convinced that God was right, and Satan was wrong. Now it is our turn to be convinced, and in heaven we will have time for all our questions to be answered.

Revelation 20:4-6: Judgment in Heaven During the Thousand Years

Verses 4 to 6 give us hints about what we will be doing during that thousand years. All God's people throughout the ages will be together for the process of looking at the records of those who did not choose to be on God's side. We know this will take place in heaven because John 14:1-3 makes it clear that Jesus will take us to heaven.

> *4 I saw thrones on which were seated those who had been given authority to judge. And I saw the souls of those who had been beheaded because of their testimony about Jesus and because of the word of God. They had not worshipped the beast or its image and had not received its mark on their foreheads or their hands. They came to life and reigned with Christ a thousand years.*
>
> *5 (The rest of the dead did not come to life until the thousand years were ended.) This is the first resurrection.*
>
> *6 Blessed and holy are those who share in the first resurrection. The second death has no power over them, but they will be priests of God and of Christ and will reign with him for a thousand years.*

This is the first resurrection which is for those who choose God's side. They are called judges and priests, and they reign with Christ. We definitely want to be a part of this group, either because we are resurrected, or even better yet, because we are still alive when Jesus comes.

Revelation 20:7-10: Satan Released

> *7 When the thousand years are over, Satan will be released from his prison*
>
> *8 and will go out to deceive the nations in the four corners of the earth—Gog and Magog—and to gather them for battle. In number they are like the sand on the seashore.*

We see in these two verses that Satan did not change his mind or his ways, even after a thousand years of nothing to do but think. As soon as he again has people to tempt, he will be right back out deceiving those who have come to life and gathering them for battle against the New Jerusalem. Those who are with him are such a huge army that he thinks there might still be a chance to take the city and win the war.

> *9 They marched across the breadth of the earth and surrounded the camp of God's people, the city he loves. But fire came down from heaven and devoured them.*

They are described as an army, marching up to the glorious city that God loves, intending to capture it. Suddenly there is a "Show and Tell." Every person will see his/her life with all the choices they made. They will see the many times and ways God tried to attract them to His side.

Finally, they will realize how Satan has deceived them so they cannot enjoy the eternity God had planned for them. In realization and remorse, they will drop to their knees acknowledging that God was not like Satan had accused Him of being.

Philippians 2:10-11, Romans 14:11-12, and Isaiah 45:23-24 all tell us that the time is coming when every knee will bow, everyone will agree that God is sovereign, He is fair, He is right, He is love, and no rebellion should ever have taken place.

> *10 And the devil, who deceived them, was thrown into the lake of burning sulfur, where the beast and the false prophet had been thrown. They will be tormented day and night for ever and ever.*

Who throws the devil into the fire? Is it the angry people who now realize how he has deceived them and kept them from eternal life? Quite likely.

We need to carefully notice something here. In verses 2 and 3 above, we saw that it was circumstances that controlled what happened. The circumstances were written in figurative language as hyperbole. Can we find figurative language and hyperbole here as well? Look at the similarities in language:

Fire came down

. . . and devoured them
(A better translation would be 'consumed them.')

The devil. . . was thrown
. . . they will be tormented (20:9b-10)

If this is hyperbole, do we find anything else in the Bible that refers to this? In Ezekiel 28:1-10 there is a prophecy about the King of Tyre who claimed to be a god. This is followed by a description that can only refer to Satan. In verse 18 it says that a fire came out from him and consumed him.

Additionally, we have one story in the Bible about the second death. It is Jesus' death on the cross. He was carrying the weight of our sins, so it could not be describing the first death. God did not kill Him. It was sin and sinners who killed Him. So that can show us something about how Satan and his followers will die. Ezekiel 28:19 says Satan will come to a horrible end and will be no more.

Revelation 20:11-15: The Last Judgment

These final verses of the chapter are scary if we don't understand them correctly. They have led people through many years to predict frightening things that could happen to us. Let's be sure we know what they are really talking about.

> *11 Then I saw a great white throne and Him who was seated on it. The earth and the heavens fled from his presence, and there was no place for them.*

Here we find more details about what happens when the huge army tries to come and take the city. This is referred to as the Great White Throne Judgment, and we can see why. God is seated on His throne and His presence is so powerful and awe inspiring that nothing else is worth paying attention to. This can also be a poetic description of the destroyed earth at this time. Remember all the destruction that took place near the time of the Second Coming, a thousand years earlier. Remember from the earlier verses of this chapter, we know that the righteous are with God and Jesus. The wicked have been brought back to life in the second resurrection. Satan and his angels have been released and are working hard to persuade everyone to attack the New Jerusalem.

If you are thinking about yourself in relationship to this event, there are only two options. If you trust in Jesus and chose to put yourself on His side, you are in the New Jerusalem and have nothing to worry about. When we study chapter 22, we will read that Jesus is coming soon and will bring His rewards with Him. (Revelation 22:12) So, if you are in heaven, you are already experiencing your reward.

In verses 4 and 6 above, we read that we will be part of the judging process during the thousand years. That cannot be judging the righteous. They have already received their reward. Their records were looked at before the Second Coming. To judge means to look at evidence. During the thousand years we will be looking at the evidence for why God could not save the people who are not in heaven at that time. We will be having all our questions answered if any family members or friends are not there enjoying heaven with us.

> *12 And I saw the dead, great and small, standing before the throne, and books were opened. Another book was opened, which is the book of life. The dead were judged according to what they had done as recorded in the books.*
>
> *13 The sea gave up the dead that were in it, and death and Hades gave up the dead that were in them, and each person was judged according to what they had done.*

This is the culmination of the judgment. Everyone throughout history who was not taken to heaven at the Second Coming, will now be resurrected in the second resurrection. They are the ones Satan is organizing to march up and take the city. God's books in heaven hold the records of everything that everyone has done. We will have had time during the thousand years to look at them and ask questions about God's decisions. Now, as the unsaved from all ages are gathered around New Jerusalem, it is their turn to look at the evidence of their lives and have their questions answered. Now is when the show and tell will happen. They will see and be reminded of all that was done by heaven to help them make the right choices. But they did not choose to be on God's side. They did not trust Him to cover them with Jesus' righteousness, and they have lost eternity.

Do you ever worry that you are not good enough to get to heaven? Well, none of us is. But we will be there because we chose Jesus to put his white robe of righteousness over us. We cannot change ourselves, but Jesus can and will gradually change us to be like Him, if we are willing to let Him do that. If there is something in your life that is separating you from Jesus, talk to Him about it and ask Him to make the needed change. Sometimes He will instantly change your mind to something better. Sometimes the change takes a long time, but you can be sure it will happen if you are putting yourself on His side every day and asking Him to forgive and transform you. While you are doing that, you are covered by Jesus' robe of righteousness. When God looks lovingly at you, He sees that Jesus' righteousness covers you. You are already saved.

What a sad, sad day that will be both outside and inside the walls of the New Jerusalem. God sent His son to undo the damage Satan had caused. The Creator and Redeemer gave His life to restore His whole family, but many rejected His efforts. The Father, Son and Holy Spirit still love all of them and are terribly sad that their place in eternity will never be filled. They will be missed forever. At last, all the unsaved will drop to their knees proclaiming that God was right all along. Their final punishment is not the fire, but the loss of an eternity of happiness and joy with Jesus and everyone else in the new earth.

> *14 Then death and Hades were thrown into the lake of fire. The lake of fire is the second death.*
>
> *15 Anyone whose name was not found written in the book of life was thrown into the lake of fire.*

This fire is in some respects figurative. It serves to remind us that after this event there will be no more death. There will never again be any need for a grave. (Hades means grave or sometimes hell. It comes from a Greek understanding of life after death which is very different from the Bible view of death as a sleep until resurrection. It was between the time of the Old and New Testaments that the Greeks conquered the world and spread their ideas everywhere.)

As we saw in the picture of wastelands at the end of chapter 19, you can be sure that fighting and killing goes on among those who now fully recognize what happened to them. They will be blaming each other. They will all be furious at Satan and his angels. How long this will go on, we cannot say, but it will not be long, and it will end with the whole earth being cleansed by fire that is hot enough to remove every vestige of sin and unrighteousness, as well as all the evidence remaining of the destroyed earth. That is the purpose of the fire—to destroy sin and cleanse the earth so it can be ready for the creation of the new earth. When it is over, only ashes will be left. (See Malachi 4:3)

Now we finally come to the last two chapters of John's vision from Jesus.

CHAPTER 21
A NEW HEAVEN AND A NEW EARTH

Revelation 21:1-8: A New Heaven and a New Earth

> *1 Then I saw "a new heaven and a new earth," for the first heaven and the first earth had passed away, and there was no longer any sea.*

Job 38 is God speaking to Job asking him questions about the time when this earth was being created. In verse 7, He mentions the reaction of the observers to that great event. ". . .while the morning stars sang together and all the angels shouted for joy. . ." In Revelation 21 we are assured that He is going to do it again, and we will be the delighted observers. The huge city will have settled on a great broad plane with a burned over surface stretching to the horizon. I'm sure we will crowd the top of the walls to get a perfect view in anticipation of what is about to happen. Our imagination is incapable of predicting the glories we will see. But I'm sure we will be singing and shouting for joy as we watch the new heaven and new earth, that have been meticulously planned and prepared, emerging from God's hands. It will be a breathtaking introduction to our forever-after life on this earth.

> *2 I saw the Holy City, the new Jerusalem, coming down out of heaven from God, prepared as a bride beautifully dressed for her husband.*

When God created the earth, He gave Adam and Eve a garden in which to live. Now as we come to the end of the story, God is giving His people a city in which to live. Is that a little strange? Not if we think carefully about it. Before sin, God visited Adam and Eve every evening. After the Exodus God told Moses to build a sanctuary so He could dwell among His people. An unnumbered multitude will gather in heaven where they will dwell with God. So, it has to be large enough for everyone who gathers there.

Let's think a bit more about a city. What history do we find in the Bible for cities? Cain built the first city (Genesis 4:17). The next reference we find is after the flood. Noah's son, Ham, had a son named Cush and a grandson named Nimrod who was a warrior and builder of cities (Genesis 10:8-12).

Ever since those questionable beginnings, cities have been places filled with rich and poor, rulers and servants, powerful and powerless and even homeless. If the pioneers intended the cities to be places of safety and abundance, they have always failed to achieve that goal for many of the inhabitants.

> *3 And I heard a loud voice from the throne saying, "Look! God's dwelling place is now among the people, and he will dwell with them. They will be his people, and God himself will be with them and be their God.*

After sin, it was no longer possible for human beings to see God. But in the New Jerusalem that separation is ended. It will be a community with no barriers. God's desire has always been to have a close relationship with His beloved children. At last, that will be reality.

> *4 He will wipe every tear from their eyes. There will be no more death or mourning or crying or pain, for the old order of things has passed away.*

All the horrors of the past will be ended. Healing will take place. During the thousand years in heaven, all questions will have been answered, and there will have been time for recovery. Body and mind and soul will be restored to wholeness. After the New Jerusalem comes down to earth and the great white throne judgement ends, all scars and memories of sin and sinners can be left behind. Suffering will have ended forever.

> 5 He who was seated on the throne said, "I am making everything new!" Then he said, "Write this down, for these words are trustworthy and true."
>
> 6 He said to me: "It is done. I am the Alpha and the Omega, the Beginning and the End. To the thirsty I will give water without cost from the spring of the water of life.
>
> 7 Those who are victorious will inherit all this, and I will be their God and they will be my children.
>
> 8 But the cowardly, the unbelieving, the vile, the murderers, the sexually immoral, those who practice magic arts, the idolaters and all liars—they will be consigned to the fiery lake of burning sulfur. This is the second death."

Probably all of us have made one or more of these bad choices at some time in our lives. We know that they cause negative feelings—mad, bad, or sad—to us and to everyone else affected by them. How wonderful that we will never experience any of that again once we are in heaven. We will all have made our final choice to totally be on Jesus' side. God didn't want anyone to miss out on eternal life. He loves even those who do not chose to be with Him. But He has to finally, sadly, leave them to the results of what they have chosen to do.

Revelation 21:9-27: The New Jerusalem, the Bride of the Lamb

> 9 One of the seven angels who had the seven bowls full of the seven last plagues came and said to me, "Come, I will show you the bride, the wife of the Lamb."

In Revelation 17:1, one of the same angels said almost the same words: "Come I will show you. . . ." That time the angel took John to see the wicked woman who had turned against God. This time the angel shows him "the bride, the wife of the Lamb." What a difference! And what a surprise! The bride is the city, the New Jerusalem. This chapter has plenty of symbols. We will list them a little bit further along. First, we will look at the description of the city, the bride. It stretches to the end of the chapter.

> *10 And he carried me away in the Spirit to a mountain great and high, and showed me the Holy City, Jerusalem, coming down out of heaven from God.*
>
> *11 It shone with the glory of God, and its brilliance was like that of a very precious jewel, like a jasper, clear as crystal.*

Everything about the city is gloriously colorful and dazzling. God who created the beautiful gemstones will use all of them to make the city totally beautiful.

> *12 It had a great, high wall with twelve gates, and with twelve angels at the gates. On the gates were written the names of the twelve tribes of Israel.*

The gates are named for the twelve sons of Israel—Jacob—from the Old Testament.

> *13 There were three gates on the east, three on the north, three on the south and three on the west.*
>
> *14 The wall of the city had twelve foundations, and on them were the names of the twelve apostles of the Lamb.*

The foundations are named for the twelve disciples of Jesus in the New Testament.

> *15 The angel who talked with me had a measuring rod of gold to measure the city, its gates and its walls.*
>
> *16 The city was laid out like a square, as long as it was wide. He measured the city with the rod and found it to be 12,000 stadia in length, and as wide and high as it is long.*

The city is as high as it is long and wide. What would you call that? A cube, of course. Each of the measurements for the Most Holy Place in Moses' tabernacle was 15 feet—width, length, and height. It did not need to be very big, because it only held one piece of furniture—the Ark—and only one man went into the room one time each year—the High Priest.

The Holy of Holies in Solomon's temple was larger, but it was still a cube. The idealized design for a temple in the book of Ezekiel was larger yet, but also a cube. And here in Revelation we find the Holy City measurement indicates a cube as well. The Holy of Holies was the place where God had His throne. In the temples on earth, that small room separated the holy from the unholy. In heaven, in the New Jerusalem, every place is holy. It is God's residence, His throne, where He will be with His people.

> *17 The angel measured the wall using human measurement, and it was 144 cubits thick.*

The measurement indicates that the wall is very thick. In our world today, walls are made high and wide and deep mostly for protection. In heaven that will not be necessary. Instead, beauty and extravagant elegance are the reason for the size and the materials used.

> *18 The wall was made of jasper, and the city of pure gold, as pure as glass.*
>
> *19 The foundations of the city walls were decorated with every kind of precious stone. The first foundation was jasper, the second sapphire, the third agate, the fourth emerald,*
>
> *20 the fifth onyx, the sixth ruby, the seventh chrysolite, the eighth beryl, the ninth topaz, the tenth turquoise, the eleventh jacinth, and the twelfth amethyst.*

We can't be sure what each of these colors look like, but there is no doubt that the foundations of the city will be full of many different gemstone colors. It is interesting that nine of these twelve jewels were worn by Lucifer when he was created. You can check out the list in Ezekiel 28:13. He was "the model of perfection" before he sinned. (verse 12) How sad that he rejected God's lofty plans for him (verse 14), and instead chose to rebel against God (verse 15).[39]

---
[39] *You can review the whole story about Lucifer/Satan in Ezekiel 28:13-19.*

21 The twelve gates were twelve pearls, each gate made of a single pearl. The great street of the city was of gold, as pure as transparent glass.

22 I did not see a temple in the city, because the Lord God Almighty and the Lamb are its temple.

23 The city does not need the sun or the moon to shine on it, for the glory of God gives it light, and the Lamb is its lamp.

24 The nations will walk by its light, and the kings of the earth will bring their splendor into it.

25 On no day will its gates ever be shut, for there will be no night there.

26 The glory and honor of the nations will be brought into it.

27 Nothing impure will ever enter it, nor will anyone who does what is shameful or deceitful, but only those whose names are written in the Lamb's book of life.

Symbols in Chapter Twenty-One

Now let's look at all the symbols found in this chapter:

New Jerusalem		
SYMBOL	MEANING—1	MEANING—2
City	People	History, culture
Bride	People	Love, intimacy
Wall and Gates	People	Twelve tribes of the sons of Israel
Foundation	People	Twelve apostles

Just as God transforms us for life in eternity, He even transforms the city into an ideal place to be living close to His people. All the symbols reflect the close fellowship between God and His people, His children, but they also show that nothing good will be lost.

Our past history will be retained in a way that confirms that God's guidance in our lives enriched us physically, mentally and spiritually while we were here on this earth. And even socially. We will not enter heaven with amnesia, but with memories intact that enhance our friendship with God. We will also recognize each other (I Corinthians 13:12).

The chapter ends, like a good love story, with a wedding. And it may surprise you to think that we are part of a symbol, because we are part of the bride. And we are part of the city because it is our history and our culture that is purified and preserved.

When the mighty city, the New Jerusalem, comes down out of heaven, all of us will come along with it because we will have been living there for the thousand years. There is an interesting passage in the Old Testament that tells us something additional about this. Because the Old Testament was written before Jesus was crucified, it shows a little different setting for the city to come down, but Zechariah 14:3-9 reveals that when Jesus comes (after the thousand years) and his feet stand on the Mount of Olives, the mountain will split in two and spread out to form a vast plain where the New Jerusalem coming down from heaven will settle. So that lets us know where on this earth the city will land.

If you would like to read a short description of this, look for the book, *Michael Asks Why*. Read the last chapter. It is only a few pages. If you want a longer description, read *Great Controversy*, Chapter 42, The Controversy Ended. Thousands of years of suffering and death and sorrow and crying are ended forever. The future of joy and fellowship and learning and creativity stretches endlessly forward.

CHAPTER 22
THE GLORIOUS CONCLUSION

We have come to the final chapter and what a joy it is to read the beautiful description of the city in which we will be living. It seems as though the Apostle John stops using symbols and just talks to us about our future.

Revelation 22:1-5: Eden Restored

> *1 Then the angel showed me the river of the water of life, as clear as crystal, flowing from the throne of God and of the Lamb*
>
> *2 down the middle of the great street of the city. On each side of the river stood the tree of life, bearing twelve crops of fruit, yielding its fruit every month. And the leaves of the tree are for the healing of the nations.*
>
> *3 No longer will there be any curse. The throne of God and of the Lamb will be in the city, and his servants will serve him.*

> *4 They will see his face, and his name will be on their foreheads.*
>
> *5 There will be no more night. They will not need the light of a lamp or the light of the sun, for the Lord God will give them light. And they will reign for ever and ever.*

God's throne is there. What do you think about when you read that? God's throne is now in heaven. Is that the center of the universe? It is fun to think about what will happen when God moves His throne. It is understandable that He wants to move, when heaven holds so many sad memories.

When we move, we just pack up and go somewhere else. When God moves, does the center of the universe also move? The results of that could be beyond our capacity to imagine. We will have to wait and see what happens, but it will be stupendous.

It is worth remembering that we will not spend all our time inside the city. We will also build homes out in the countryside as well. Isaiah 65:22 tells us we will build houses and plant vineyards. But the New Jerusalem will always be our city. We will go there on Sabbath to worship, and other times for special events (Isaiah 66:22-23). It seems that human beings who went through the time of Satan's rebellion are privileged to live the closest to God and Jesus.

Revelation 22:6-11: John and the Angel

> *6 The angel said to me, "These words are trustworthy and true. The Lord, the God who inspires the prophets, sent his angel to show his servants the things that must soon take place."*
>
> *7 "Look, I am coming soon! Blessed is the one who keeps the words of the prophecy written in this scroll."*
>
> *8 I, John, am the one who heard and saw these things. And when I had heard and seen them, I fell down to worship at the feet of the angel who had been showing them to me.*

> 9 But he said to me, "Don't do that! I am a fellow servant with you and with your fellow prophets and with all who keep the words of this scroll. Worship God!"
>
> 10 Then he told me, "Do not seal up the words of the prophecy of this scroll, because the time is near.
>
> 11 Let the one who does wrong continue to do wrong; let the vile person continue to be vile; let the one who does right continue to do right; and let the holy person continue to be holy."

Epilogue: Invitation and Warning

> 12 "Look, I am coming soon! My reward is with me, and I will give to each person according to what they have done.
>
> 13 I am the Alpha and the Omega, the First and the Last, the Beginning and the End.
>
> 14 "Blessed are those who wash their robes, that they may have the right to the tree of life and may go through the gates into the city.
>
> 15 Outside are the dogs, those who practice magic arts, the sexually immoral, the murderers, the idolaters and everyone who loves and practices falsehood.

One more time we read that everything in heaven will be clean and pure and lovely. There won't be anyone to be afraid of, or anyone doing harmful things that hurt other people or cause us to have negative feelings. It is hard to even imagine such a perfect world, but we will be living with Jesus and experiencing it. What a glorious thought!

> 16 "I, Jesus, have sent my angel to give you this testimony for the churches. I am the Root and the Offspring of David, and the bright Morning Star."

One last time Jesus reminds us that He is the one who sent this message. It is like He is saying, "Take care. I love you. I wanted you to know these things so you would be ready to come and live with Me. I'll see you soon. It will be wonderful having you here with Me."

> *17 The Spirit and the bride say, "Come!" And let the one who hears say, "Come!" Let the one who is thirsty come; and let the one who wishes take the free gift of the water of life.*

The Holy Spirit is inviting people to come. And the bride is also inviting people to come. Remember that we are part of the bride. Plus, everyone who hears will be inviting people to come. That again is us. We have the privilege of sharing the good news with others, so as many people as possible can enjoy eternity with Jesus and with us.

> *18 I warn everyone who hears the words of the prophecy of this scroll: If anyone adds anything to them, God will add to that person the plagues described in this scroll.*

> *19 And if anyone takes words away from this scroll of prophecy, God will take away from that person any share in the tree of life and in the Holy City, which are described in this scroll.*

In the two verses above, Jesus is warning us not to make changes in this book. He wants us to study and learn to understand it, but don't try to change the meaning in any way that would make it harder for people to understand the message that is here.

> *20 He who testifies to these things says, "Yes, I am coming soon."*

These are Jesus' final words: "I'll be coming soon to take you with me."

And we respond: "Amen. Come, Lord Jesus."

And John the Apostle who wrote the book adds his farewell blessing to us:

> *21 The grace of the Lord Jesus be with God's people. Amen.*

The End.

APPENDIX A

Biblical Research Institute, Reflections #87
Chart: The Sabbath and the Mark of the Beast

SABBATH	MARK OF THE BEAST
1. Related to worship	*1. Related to worship*
"**Worship** Him who made the heaven and the earth and the sea and the spring of waters" (Rev 14:7).	"Those who **worship** the beast… and whoever receives the mark of his name" (Rev 14:9).
2. Related to a name	*2. Related to a name*
"Having His [the **Lamb**'s] name and the name of His **Father** written on their foreheads" (Rev 14:1; cf. Exod 20:11).	"Whoever receives the mark of **his name**" (Rev 14:11); a mark on his forehead or on his hand (Rev 14:9).
3. Related to a number	*3. Related to a number*
"He rested on the **seventh** day" (Gen 2:2).	"The mark…of the beast or the number of his name…**666**" (Rev 13:17–18).
4. Given to humankind	*4. Forced on humankind*
"The Sabbath was made for **man/ humankind**" (Mark 2:27).	"And he causes **all**…to be given a mark on their right hand…" (Rev 13:16).
5. Uses language of buying and selling	*5. Uses language of buying and selling*
"…any grain on the Sabbath day to **sell**, we will not buy on the Sabbath" (Neh 10:31).	"…no one will be able to **buy** or to **sell** except the one who has the mark" (Rev 13:17).
…	…

6. Sign of identity: followers of the Lamb

"[They] follow the Lamb wherever He goes" (Rev 14:4; cf. Ezek 20:20).

7. Sign of submission to God

"until we have sealed the **bondservants** of our God on their foreheads" (Rev 7:3).

8. Rejection leads to idolatry

"Profane My Sabbaths…**went after the idols**" (Ezek 20:16).

9. Rejecters

"Everyone who profanes it shall surely be **put to death**" (Exod 31:14).

6. Sign of identity: followers of the beast

"Whoever receives the mark of his name" (Rev 14:11); "the whole earth was amazed and followed after the beast" (Rev 13:3).

7. Sign of submission to the beast

"Buy or sell… **except the one** who has the mark" (Rev 13:17).

8. Sign of idolatry (an image)

"If anyone **worships** the beast and his **image**, receives a mark" (Rev 14:9).

9. Rejecters

Ordered "to **be killed**" (Rev 13:15).

Ángel Manuel Rodriquez

Retired Director of the Biblical Research Institute

BIBLIOGRAPHY

Andrews Study Bible, NIV. (2019). Berrien Springs, MI: Andrews University Press.

Badenas, Roberto. (1992). New Jerusalem – The Holy City. In F. B. Holbrook (Ed.), Symposium on Revelation–Book II. Daniel and Revelation committee series (vol. 7, pp. 243-274). Silver Spring, MD: Biblical Research Institute, General Conference of Seventh-day Adventists.

Badina, Joel. (1992). The Millennium. In F. B. Holbrook (Ed.), Symposium on Revelation–Book II. Daniel and Revelation committee series (vol. 7, pp. 225-242). Silver Spring, MD: Biblical Research Institute, General Conference of Seventh-day Adventists.

Bible Gateway. https://www.biblegatewaycom quicksearch/?quicksearch=Revelation&version=NIV

Davidson, Richard M. (1992). Sanctuary Typology. In F. B. Holbrook (Ed.), Symposium on Revelation–Book I. Daniel and Revelation committee series (vol. 6, pp. 99-130). Silver Spring, MD: Biblical Research Institute, General Conference of Seventh-day Adventists.

Dillon, Sally Pierson. (2000). Michael Asks Why. Mountain View, CA: Pacific Press Association.

Dillon, Sally, and Smith, Virginia (1997). Making the Bible a Delight! A Guide to Bible Study with Children. Hagerstown, MD: Review and Herald Graphics.

Heinz, Johann. (1992). The Modern Papacy: Claims and Authority. In F. B. Holbrook (Ed.), Symposium on Revelation–Book II. Daniel and Revelation committee series (vol. 7, pp. 335-372). Silver Spring, MD: Biblical Research Institute, General Conference of Seventh-day Adventists.

Johnsson, William G. (1992). The Saints' End-Time Victory Over the Forces of Evil. In F. B. Holbrook (Ed.), Symposium on Revelation–Book II. Daniel and Revelation committee series (vol. 7, pp. 3-40). Silver Spring, MD: Biblical Research Institute, General Conference of Seventh-day Adventists.

Kiesler, Herbert. (1992). Christ: Son of Man: Lamb. In F. B. Holbrook (Ed.), Symposium on Revelation–Book II. Daniel and Revelation committee series (vol. 7, pp. 409-432). Silver Spring, MD: Biblical Research Institute, General Conference of Seventh-day Adventists.

Ladd, George Elden. (1956). The Blessed Hope. Grand Rapids, MI: Eerdmans.

Ladd, George Eldon. (2018). A Commentary on the Revelation of John. Grand Rapids, MI: Eerdmans.

LaRondelle, Hans K. (1992). Armageddon: History of Adventist Interpretations. In F. B. Holbrook (Ed.), Symposium on Revelation–Book II. Daniel and Revelation committee series (vol. 7, pp. 435-450). Silver Spring, MD: Biblical Research Institute, General Conference of Seventh-day Adventists.

LaRondelle, Hans K. (1992). Armageddon: Sixth and Seventh Plagues. In F. B. Holbrook (Ed.), Symposium on Revelation–Book II. Daniel and Revelation committee series (vol. 7, pp. 373-390). Silver Spring, MD: Biblical Research Institute, General Conference of Seventh-day Adventists.

LaRondelle, Hans K. (1992). Babylon: Anti-Christian Empire. In F. B. Holbrook (Ed.), Symposium on Revelation–Book II. Daniel and Revelation committee series (vol. 7, pp. 151-176). Silver Spring, MD: Biblical Research Institute, General Conference of Seventh-day Adventists.

LaRondelle, Hans K. (1992). Contextual Approach to the Seven last Plagues. In F. B. Holbrook (Ed.), Symposium on Revelation–Book II. Daniel and Revelation committee series (vol. 7, pp. 133-150). Silver Spring, MD: Biblical Research Institute, General Conference of Seventh-day Adventists.

Lehmann, Richard. (1992). Relationships Between Daniel and Revelation. In F. B. Holbrook (Ed.), Symposium on Revelation–Book I. Daniel and Revelation committee series (vol. 6, pp. 131-144). Silver Spring, MD: Biblical Research Institute, General Conference of Seventh-day Adventists.

Lehmann, Richard. (1992). The Two Suppers. In F. B. Holbrook (Ed.), Symposium on Revelation–Book II. Daniel and Revelation committee series (vol. 7, pp. 207-224). Silver Spring, MD: Biblical Research Institute, General Conference of Seventh-day Adventists.

Lesher, W. Richard & Holbrook, Frank B. (1992). Daniel and Revelation Committee: Final Report. In F. B. Holbrook (Ed.), Symposium on Revelation–Book II. Daniel and Revelation committee series (vol. 7, pp. 451-460). Silver Spring, MD: Biblical Research Institute, General Conference of Seventh-day Adventists.

Maxwell, C. Mervyn. (1992). Note on Elthen (Has Come). In F. B. Holbrook (Ed.), Symposium on Revelation–Book II. Daniel and Revelation committee series (vol. 7, pp. 433-434). Silver Spring, MD: Biblical Research Institute, General Conference of Seventh-day Adventists.

Maxwell, C. Mervyn. (1992). The Mark of the Beast. In F. B. Holbrook (Ed.), Symposium on Revelation–Book II. Daniel and Revelation committee series (vol. 7, pp. 41-132). Silver Spring, MD: Biblical Research Institute, General Conference of Seventh-day Adventists.

Neall, Beatrice. (1992). Sealed Saints and the Tribulation. In F. B. Holbrook (Ed.), Symposium on Revelation–Book I. Daniel and Revelation committee series (vol. 6, pp. 245-278). Silver Spring, MD: Biblical Research Institute, General Conference of Seventh-day Adventists.

Paulien, Jon (1992). Interpreting Revelation's Symbolism. In F. B. Holbrook (Ed.), Symposium on Revelation–Book I. Daniel and Revelation committee series (vol. 6, pp. 73-98). Silver Spring, MD: Biblical Research Institute, General Conference of Seventh-day Adventists.

Paulien, Jon. (1992). Ellen G. White and Revelation 4-6. In F. B. Holbrook (Ed.), Symposium on Revelation–Book I. Daniel and Revelation committee series (vol. 6, pp. 363-374). Silver Spring, MD: Biblical Research Institute, General Conference of Seventh-day Adventists.

Paulien, Jon. (1992). Seals and Trumpets: Some Current Discussions. In F. B. Holbrook (Ed.), Symposium on Revelation–Book I. Daniel and Revelation committee series (vol. 6, pp. 183-198). Silver Spring, MD: Biblical Research Institute, General Conference of Seventh-day Adventists.

Paulien, Jon. (1992). The Interpreter's Use of the Writings of Ellen G. White. In F. B. Holbrook (Ed.), Symposium on Revelation–Book I. Daniel and Revelation committee series (vol. 6, pp. 163-174). Silver Spring, MD: Biblical Research Institute, General Conference of Seventh-day Adventists.

Paulien, Jon. (1992). The Seven Seals. In F. B. Holbrook (Ed.), Symposium on Revelation–Book I. Daniel and Revelation committee series (vol. 6, pp. 199-244). Silver Spring, MD: Biblical Research Institute, General Conference of Seventh-day Adventists.

Paulsen, Jan. (1992). Sanctuary and Judgment. In F. B. Holbrook (Ed.), Symposium on Revelation–Book II. Daniel and Revelation committee series (vol. 7, pp. 275-294). Silver Spring, MD: Biblical Research Institute, General Conference of Seventh-day Adventists.

Pfandl, Gerhard. (1992). The Remnant Church and the Spirit of Prophecy. In F. B. Holbrook (Ed.), Symposium on Revelation–Book II. Daniel and Revelation committee series (vol. 7, pp. 295-334). Silver Spring, MD: Biblical Research Institute, General Conference of Seventh-day Adventists.

Rice, George E. (1992). Ellen G. White's Use of Daniel and Revelation. In F. B. Holbrook (Ed.), Symposium on Revelation–Book I. Daniel and Revelation committee series (vol. 6, pp. 145-162). Silver Spring, MD: Biblical Research Institute, General Conference of Seventh-day Adventists.

Rodriquez, Angel Manuel (2024) "The Eschatological Role of the Sabbath: Some Reflections," *Reflections*, September, 2-5.

Shea, William H. (1992). Sabbath Hymns for the Heavenly Sanctuary (Qumran). In F. B. Holbrook (Ed.), Symposium on Revelation–Book II. Daniel and Revelation committee series (vol. 7, pp. 391-408). Silver Spring, MD: Biblical Research Institute, General Conference of Seventh-day Adventists.

Shea, William H. (1992). The Mighty Angel and His Message. In F. B. Holbrook (Ed.), Symposium on Revelation–Book I. Daniel and Revelation committee series (vol. 6, pp. 279-326). Silver Spring, MD: Biblical Research Institute, General Conference of Seventh-day Adventists.

Shea, William H. (1992). Time Prophecies of Daniel 12 and Revelation 12-13. In F. B. Holbrook (Ed.), Symposium on Revelation–Book I. Daniel and Revelation committee series (vol. 6, pp. 327-362). Silver Spring, MD: Biblical Research Institute, General Conference of Seventh-day Adventists.

Shea, William H. (1992). When Did the Seventy Weeks of Daniel 9:24 Begin? In F. B. Holbrook (Ed.), Symposium on Revelation–Book I. Daniel and Revelation committee series (vol. 6, pp. 375-394). Silver Spring, MD: Biblical Research Institute, General Conference of Seventh-day Adventists.

Sigve Tonstad, 33 min. Re-Reading Revelation, Lecture 7: ...and to the One Who Has an Ear, 2020. YouTube.

Sigve Tonstad, 35 min. Re-Reading Revelation, Lecture 1: Retrieving the Vision of Healing, 2020. YouTube.

Sigve Tonstad, 35 min. Re-Reading Revelation, Lecture 4: How to Read Revelation, 2020. YouTube.

Sigve Tonstad, 37 min. Re-Reading Revelation, Lecture # 8: Open Heaven, 2021. YouTube.

Sigve Tonstad, 40 min. Re-Reading Revelation, Lecture 5: Incentive to Read, 2020. YouTube.

Sigve Tonstad, 42 min. Re-Reading Revelation, Lecture # 9: Crisis in the Heavenly Council, 2021. YouTube.

Sigve Tonstad, 44 min. Re-Reading Revelation, Lecture 2: Approaches to Revelation, 2020. YouTube.

Sigve Tonstad, 44 min. Re-Reading Revelation, Lecture 6: To the Seven Believing Communities, 2020. YouTube.

Sigve Tonstad, 45 min. Re-Reading Revelation, Lecture 3: Who, What, Where, When, and Why, 2020. YouTube.

Sigve Tonstad, 46 min. Re-Reading Revelation, Lecture # 14: Message and Mission in the Trumpets, 2021. YouTube.

Sigve Tonstad, 46 min. Re-Reading Revelation, Lecture # 15: Message and Method in the Trumpets, 2021. YouTube.

Sigve Tonstad, 47:42 min. Re-Reading Revelation, Lecture # 20: The Seven Bowls, 2023. YouTube.

Sigve Tonstad, 50 min. Re-Reading Revelation, Lecture # 10: Breaking the Seals, 2021. YouTube.

Sigve Tonstad, 50 min. Re-Reading Revelation, Lecture # 16: The Cosmic Conflict from A to Z, Part I, 2021. YouTube.

Sigve Tonstad, 51:05 min. Re-Reading Revelation, Lecture # 23: War, Wedding, and Wasteland, 2023. YouTube.

Sigve Tonstad, 51:20 min. Re-Reading Revelation, Lecture # 21: The Beast That Was and Is Not and Is to Come, 2021. YouTube.

Sigve Tonstad, 51:20 min. Re-Reading Revelation, Lecture # 21: The Beast That Was and Is Not and Is to Come, 2023. YouTube.

Sigve Tonstad, 51:28 min. Re-Reading Revelation, Lecture # 22: Babylon Undone (new recording), 2023. YouTube.

Sigve Tonstad, 52 min. Re-Reading Revelation, Lecture # 11: The Sealing and the Seventh Seal, 2021. Youtube.

Sigve Tonstad, 52:45 min. Re-Reading Revelation, Lecture # 17: The Cosmic Conflict from A to Z. Part II-1. The Dragon Acts, 2021. YouTube.

Sigve Tonstad, 52:45 min. Re-Reading Revelation, Lecture # 18: The Cosmic Conflict from A to Z. Part II-2. The Dragon Acts, 2021. YouTube.

Sigve Tonstad, 52:45 min. Re-Reading Revelation, Lecture # 19: The Cosmic Conflict from A to Z, Part III, 2021. YouTube.

Sigve Tonstad, 53 min. Re-Reading Revelation, Lecture # 12: The Seven Trumpets, 2021. YouTube.

Sigve Tonstad, 57:36 min. Re-Reading Revelation, Lecture # 24: The Thousand Years and Then, 2023. YouTube.

Sigve Tonstad, 58 min. Re-Reading Revelation, Lecture # 13: The Quest for History in the Seven Trumpets, 2021. YouTube.

Stefanovic, Ranko. (2020). "Revelation." In Andrews Bible Commentary Light, Depth, Truth. New Testament, edited by Angel Manuel Rodriguez. Berrien Springs, MI: Andrews University Press.

Strand, Kenneth A. (1992). The Seven Heads: Do They Represent Roman Emperors? In F. B. Holbrook (Ed.), Symposium on Revelation–book II. Daniel and Revelation committee series (vol. 7, pp. 177-206). Silver Spring, MD: Biblical Research Institute, General Conference of Seventh-day Adventists.

Strand, Kenneth A. (1992). Foundational Principles of Interpretation. In F. B. Holbrook (Ed.), Symposium on Revelation–Book 1. Daniel and Revelation committee series (vol. 6, pp. 3-34). Silver Spring, MD: Biblical Research Institute, General Conference of Seventh-day Adventists.

Strand, Kenneth A. (1992). The Eight Basic Visions. In F. B. Holbrook (Ed.), Symposium on Revelation–Book I. Daniel and Revelation committee series (vol. 6, pp. 35-50). Silver Spring, MD: Biblical Research Institute, General Conference of Seventh-day Adventists.

Strand, Kenneth A. (1992). Victorious-Introductio Scenes. In F. B. Holbrook (Ed.), Symposium on Revelation–Book I. Daniel and Revelation committee series (vol. 6, pp. 51-72). Silver Spring, MD: Biblical Research Institute, General Conference of Seventh-day Adventists.

Tonstad, Sigve. (2019). Revelation (Paideia: Commentaries on the New Testament). Grand Rapids, MI: Baker Academic.

Voerman, Jan. (2009). "The Reign of Terror." Andrews University Seminary Studies Vol. 47, No. 1, 117-134.

White, Ellen G. (1882). Early Writings of Ellen G. White. Washington, D.C.: Review and Herald.

White, Ellen G. (1898). The Desire of Ages. Mountain View, CA: Pacific Press.

White, Ellen G. (1901). Testimonies for the Church, Volume 6. Mountain View, CA: Pacific Press.

White, Ellen G. (1903). Education. Mountain View, CA: Pacific Press.

White, Ellen G. (1911). The Great Controversy Between Christ and Satan. Mountain View, CA: Pacific Press.

White, Ellen G. (1917). Prophets and Kings. Mountain View, CA: Pacific Press.

White, Ellen G. (1923). Testimonies to Ministers and Gospel Workers. Mountain View, CA: Pacific Press.

White, Ellen G. (1946). Evangelism. Washington, D.C.: Review and Herald.

Winn, Laura Rocke. (1999). Margie Asks, Why Do People Have to Die? Hagerstown, MD: Review and Herald

ABOUT THE AUTHOR

Virginia Lorene Schuler Smith has had a lifetime of teaching. As she finished her B.A. in English, it occurred to her that maybe she should take one education class, just in case she needed to teach. Three or four years later she began putting that information to use when she taught high school at Ikizu Adventist Secondary School in Tanzania. She also home schooled her own two children because there was not classroom space for all the Tanzanian children who needed an education.

Moving to Singapore, she completed two master's degrees and then taught as an Assistant Professor in Southeast Asia Union College. While teaching, she completed all the education classes needed to achieve teaching credentials for both elementary and secondary levels. Next, she worked as a graduate Assistant in Michigan State University while completing the coursework for a PhD.

For 13 years she was Children's Ministries Director at the General Conference of Seventh-day Adventists, holding seminars in 73 countries as well as editing up to nine quarterly publications for children's Sabbath schools. The first three years she shifted gears every night at 6 pm to work on her dissertation, finally finishing on October 22, 1993. That is a hard date to forget!

After leaving that job to care for three elderly parents, she also held seminars, classes, and evangelistic meetings in various local churches, and served as a school board chairman, a television station board chairman, the board secretary for a local senior citizen center, and elder and treasurer in local churches.

Her specialty was the book of Daniel, but when urged, she also held Revelation seminars. She was not satisfied that the true meaning of the book was understood until she encountered Dr. Sigve Tonstad's book, Revelation, and then began watching his Revelation class on YouTube. The fresh insights were so motivating that she began contemplating a similar book for young people.

. . .

About the Author

There are three kinds of thinkers. Those who study deeply into new theories and ways of understanding information; second, those who need to know the new information but will seldom or never read the scholarly books that contain it; and finally, a small third group who do read and study, then put it into language that the second group can become excited about. Dr. Virginia likes to think of herself as one of the members of the third group. Her desire is to share great ideas with the second group in simplified language that draws them into the conversation about new ways of thinking and better understanding.

PUBLICATIONS

Educating Thinkers in Sabbath School

Making the Bible a Delight, with Sally Dillon

What in the World Happened in the Kingdom of Judah? The life and times of Isaiah the Prophet, with Jessica Dill

Edited *Islam in Focus: History, Doctrine, & Philosophy*

Edited *Islamic Culture & Society*

Edited *The First Hundred Years of the SDA Church in China* (1600 pages)

Semi-Ghost writer for *My Life Stories*, by Calvin Lloyd Smith

www.ingramcontent.com/pod-product-compliance
Lightning Source LLC
Chambersburg PA
CBHW032107090426
42743CB00007B/272